PROMISES KEPT

Stories of How Wise Financial Decisions Provided a Secure Future

www.promiseskeptbook.com

PROMISES KEPT

ISBN 978-0-615-32932-1

Printed in the United States of America

Published by International Educational Finance Institute, LLC
Two Greentree Centre
Suite 300
Marlton, NJ 08053

Promises Kept is an account written by financial advisors themselves about their work with certain clients. As of the publication of Promises Kept, many of the contributors were registered representatives and/or investment advisor representatives of Mutual of Omaha Investor Services, a securities broker dealer and registered investment advisor, member FINRA. Home Office, Mutual of Omaha Plaza, Omaha, NE 68175-1020. Contributors Chris Casey, Tony Engrassia, Mike Herman, Marty Higgins, Kevin Pearce, Danny Smith, Kevin Swan, Dana Troske and Jay Van Beusekom were registered representatives and investment advisor representatives of Mutual of Omaha Investor Services. Mike Collins and Andy Rodriguez were registered representatives of Mutual of Omaha Investor Services, but not investment advisor representatives. These representatives only conduct business in states in which they are registered. Products and services referred to in this book may not be available in all states or to all clients. Mutual of Omaha Investor Services and its associated persons do not give tax or legal advice.

The information and opinions in this book are the information and opinions of the respective contributors, provided for information purposes only, and not offered as a solicitation to buy or sell any of the products referred to in the text. This information should not be used as the single source of information for making any financial decision, including the decision to buy any of the products or services referred to in the book, or to work with any of the persons referred to in this book. Please seek the advice of appropriate professionals regarding any specific content.

Foreword

It was as a college student that I learned the value and importance of life insurance ownership. In 1953, as a junior in college, I started selling life insurance. It was my privilege to attend Illinois Wesleyan University where Life Insurance was taught as a three-hour course. Dr. William T. Beadles was the Professor of Insurance and a prime mover in the American College of Life Underwriters. He was not only an effective teacher and professor, but he was also a real believer in the product of Life Insurance.

My brother, Jack, and I took several insurance courses under Dr. Beadles, including the three-hour course in Life Insurance. Upon entering the life insurance business in Bloomington, Illinois, I took my CLU instruction under this great professor, Dr. William T. Beadles. He, along with Solomon Huebner, graded the first CLU exams taken in the United States.

Together, they were the creators of the Human Life Value approach to buying life insurance. We were taught that people should buy life insurance to protect ten years of income, twenty years of income or income to age sixty-five. In addition, there should be enough additional life insurance to take care of any debt the family or business might have at the time of death. This is how the Human Life Value concept got its start in the United States.

Dr. Beadles taught us to buy as much permanent life insurance as the company would issue. He was a real believer in permanent life insurance. He believed in buying as much as you possibly could and doing it as young as you could.

With this background and education at Illinois Wesleyan University, my brother and I started our careers in the life insurance business. Jack started in our hometown of Pekin, Illinois and I got my start in Bloomington, our college town. Over 50 years later it is still my passion to promulgate the buying of permanent life insurance.

When I was asked to write the introduction to this book entitled, *Promises Kept*, I was reminded that life insurance is all about promises. The client promises to pay the premium and the insurance company promises to provide value to families at a time when it is needed most.

The great thing about life insurance is that it is impossible to pay in the face amount all the way up to the issue age of 70. At all the ages up to the age of 70 it is virtually impossible for the client to pay in what they are covered for from day one.

It is exciting to me to know that the client, instantly, miraculously creates an estate for **$1,000,000** with a premium of only $24,000 a year. Let me give you an example: A client starts a program at age 40 where they pay premiums of $24,000 until age 65 (25 years) and then stop. That is $24,000 a year for 25 years, totaling $600,000. This means they can never pay in what they are covered for from day one. **What a tremendous financial product!**

In addition, if you buy whole life and the whole life is participating, the dividends paid to the policyholder are buying paid-up insurance. The amount of life insurance keeps increasing every year starting with the third year. The cash value also continues to increase.

The people reading this book will benefit greatly as consumers of the finest financial product ever devised by the mind of man.

Garry D. Kinder, CLU, RFC
CEO
The KBI Group
www.KBIgroup.com

INTRODUCTION

The following is a recent interview I did as we put the final touches on this book. I thought it would make a great introduction. I hope you enjoy reading it

Marty Higgins
December 2009

HOST: So Marty tell me a little bit about what is Promises Kept about?

MARTY: The book's purpose is to create a collection of feel good stories, kind of like a Chicken Soup for the Soul series, where people can read these stories and see themselves in there and feel good about different financial decisions that they may be contemplating based on the stories of what others have done. So they're going to look at past successes, at what advisors have done for people, how they've helped them and be able to relate to those situations and stories to their own situation.

HOST: So, Marty, Promises Kept is really about real life experiences that advisors have gone through. This is not fiction. This is I guess what they say, "fact is truer than fiction." So these are real life experiences that have actually happened to people. Is that correct?

MARTY: That's correct. Right from the financial advisors' own experience of an actual anonymous client.

HOST: Now, Marty, what inspired you to create a book like Promises Kept?

MARTY: Clearly good news doesn't sell. If you're walking by a newsstand and saw a magazine that said everything is okay you're not going to buy it. If you see a headline, and it says "Learn the Five Ways You're Getting Ripped Off by Your Financial Advisor"u might spend a couple of bucks to buy that magazine. So bad news sells, good news doesn't and so it never gets the media's attention, but it's really enriched people's lives by what honest and ethical financial advisors do for a living, whether it be bringing a check to a widow that can stay in her home and send her kids to college, to another advisor who would bring a check to a business owner so the business can stay in place and the employees can keep their jobs all the way to paying medical bills or long-term care nursing home or assisted living expenses so that the surviving spouse doesn't have to go on welfare and move in with her kids. So there are a lot of good things that are being done and people need to know about it. They need to know and understand how these products work and how good financial advisors help people.

HOST: So when I say real life experiences, it sounds to me like Promises Kept is about the emotional side and the inspirational side of what an advisor would do and how that interaction takes place perhaps under the duress of a death or a disability or some other type of life event that would cause financial and even emotional concern for clients.

MARTY: Exactly. It shows the power of planning, how a promise made maybe 10, 15, 20 years ago or more is kept today when that unexpected event, life-changing event may happen to someone good you know. Bad things happen to good people so these are the stories, the real life stories of actual financial advisors and their experiences in dealing with families, individuals and businesses.

HOST: I love your term Marty, "The Power of Planning" because as advisors we know we don't create problems we create solutions, and I'm wondering how can Promises Kept help people, help our clients identify the dangers, the financial dangers if you will, that they may face in the future?

MARTY: Well I think people, adults in particular, will learn from stories. People relate to stories when they can see themselves inside them. They can picture it versus looking at just a lot of really confusing charts and graphs with numbers and just stuff that you know an individual's eyes glaze over, so stories help to pull people in. They can see themselves in that story. They can see that situation happening to them and from a conceptual standpoint that allows them to understand how that product or service can help them and better their situation, better their lives.

HOST: You know that's interesting. I'm wondering with the multiple contributing authors that are going to be part of the Promises Kept book I'm certain that there have to be many stories from many different angles. Marty, tell me a little bit about some of the contributing authors and maybe their background or what you know about them.

MARTY: Well they're all financial advisors with a level of experience that I would say covers anywhere from probably 5 to about 35 years. These are people with some amazing stories. We personally screened all of these individuals to make sure that they had something in their background where they really had a life changing experience with one of their clients or they had the unfortunate opportunity to bring a check to a widow or help somebody who is disabled and initiate that claim, make sure that they had a check coming in to pay the mortgage and buy food and things like that, somebody who has been in the business long enough to have had an experience to help somebody that would be of value to the book. So the purpose is to communicate planning across a different spectrum, whether it be life insurance, disability insurance, long-term care, maybe even just financial planning in general. We also have some tips from other advisors like CPAs and Attorneys in the book from their perspective on things an individual should be doing for planning. So it's going to cover different areas of planning across a broad spectrum of experiences.

HOST: Well that's interesting because Promises Kept is going to be based on things that have actually happened not things that an advisor has heard about or a story that they might have heard when they went out to a home office training. These are actual real life experiences that really brought together the advisor and his or her clients and how that decision, that planning decision that was made earlier impacted the lives of the family of the clients that were involved with the various advisors. Is that pretty well what you're trying to accomplish with Promises Kept?

MARTY: Absolutely. This isn't hearsay. This is the actual real life experiences of those advisors. So I think that in some stories you'll be able to almost see yourself in that situation as if you're sitting in the room.

HOST: And when we get involved with the insurance side of things or the financial side of things and again as I always say under duress I mean you just can't make up things that happen when the unexpected happens and when an unthinkable event happens, the death of a mom or a dad, I mean all the training in the world just doesn't bring home the impact that we as an advisor might be faced with in working with the families. In this book each chapter sounds to me like it is going to be kind of a synopsis of that particular event and the real people that were involved in whatever was taking place at that time.

MARTY: That's right, and I think those are real people that you don't get to hear about because the media doesn't promote it as newsworthy because it doesn't sell. We just want to tell the public that there are good people out there in this business. They're not all on Dateline or 60 Minutes and you know they do good things for good people and the public needs to know about it.

HOST: Now that's interesting because if an advisor or an insurance agent brings a check for $500,000 or $1 million to a widow and her children that's just not going to get on any media radar and that's really what it's all about, it's the real core of what advisors do in helping families through those very difficult times.

MARTY: That's absolutely right and as excellent financial advisors that is our purpose.

HOST: So the motto, I guess the morale of the story is that people can learn from stories, from actual events and that stories are important to people and that we can all learn something new. We've all learned in the past that there's a morale behind even the simplest stories or the fairytale stories we hear as kids. Some of that goes into the heart and I guess you can put that to use and maybe <u>Promises Kept</u> will be able to do that for a lot of people we hope.

MARTY: I sincerely hope so.

Contents

Luck Be A Lady

By Martin V. Higgins, CFP

Back in the mid-'90s, one of the most effective ways that I marketed my financial planning practice was to co-host educational workshops. My goal with each workshop was to make sure everyone was well informed about the importance of planning for the future. I always teamed up with a well-known estate planning attorney who would co-present on their area of expertise. Together, we'd touch on topics like wills and trusts, long-term care, and multi-generational IRA planning.

We would meet with the clients initially together, then meet separately to go into more detail about a particular topic that they wanted to discuss. What attendees enjoyed most about these seminars was that the attorney and I worked as a team. Instead of working separately, solely in our own area, we came together and painted the entire financial picture for them and how it all intertwined — not just our little piece. It was at one of these seminars where I first met Don and Kay.

Soon thereafter, I began working with Don and Kay to assist them in planning for their future. We started the relationship by repositioning their portfolio to include more asset classes and provide more meaningful diversification to reduce their overall risk. I also referred them to a new CPA because I saw they weren't getting the proper advice on their taxes.

Several years went by this way, and then one day I received a call from the CPA. He informed me that Don and Kay were on their way to see me. When I asked why, his response remained mysterious, "I'll let them tell you for themselves."

As it turns out Don and Kay had visited the casino over the weekend and, while playing the quarter slots, had managed to win $777,000. A huge windfall!

Don and Kay didn't live an extravagant lifestyle, so their winnings acted like "longevity insurance." If they needed the money it was there, but their main goal was preserving their winnings for their children to have once they were gone.

With this new money and their primary goal of legacy in mind, I went to work to maximize their financial portfolio. First, we opened up a managed money account with a third-party investment firm. Second, we invested in a variable annuity that offered a five percent growth on the death benefits. This meant every year they were guaranteed that the death benefit would grow a minimum of five percent, regardless of how the stock market performed. If the market did better than five percent, they would receive the greater amount. Don and Kay felt comfortable with this option. It not only preserved their money for their heirs, but also allowed it the opportunity to grow.

A few years later, I was on my way home from a conference in San Diego when I learned that Don had passed away. Instead of going home, I made the drive to Princeton to attend the viewing. Don and Kay had four children, a son and three daughters. I'd met the son before but never the daughters. After a brief introduction to one of the daughters, she said right in front of me, "Mom, I've read that you're not supposed to make any financial decisions for at least three to six months, until your mind is clearer and you're less emotional."

Kay responded, “Oh, no, Honey. Daddy and I have been working with Marty for several years, and I know exactly what we’re doing financially.”

Eureka! That’s it! I’d been in this business for a long time, but it was at that very moment that I realized how valuable financial planning truly is. Planning allows for a widow (Kay) to stand there and grieve for the loss of her husband, but not have to worry about money. She and Don took the steps together in advance to ensure that everything would be handled properly.

One of the difficulties with their generation (those in their 60s and 70s) is that traditionally, the husband handled all of the financial decisions. This left the wife financially clueless. Moreover as this generation matures, I find that the husbands are troubled about what will happen to their wives financially should they pass away first. Would the wife cash in all the stocks and go running to the bank and purchase the “super CD” because she didn’t understand (or care to understand) finances? This concern is worrisome and draining for the husband. He wants to ensure that his wife is taken care of financially, and that their legacy is passed onto their children and perhaps even their grandchildren.

One of the biggest benefits of financial planning is that when couples plan together for the future, they remove the worry and replace it with peace of mind. When both the husband and the wife express their wishes, financial planning can be extremely freeing for couples, and they are able to enjoy their golden years together, knowing that their financial house is in order.

After Don's death, Kay and I got together and reviewed the estate, looked at her cash flow, and determined how much she needed to live comfortably. Now that there was ample money available, we set up a trust for Don's estate that could stay in deferral indefinitely and also grow, free of federal estate taxes. This would be the legacy that Don and Kay would leave their children.

A few years later during an annual review, Kay indicated that she wanted to maximize the estate for her heirs. She was living comfortably, and one of her concerns was the estate tax burden her kids would be faced with upon her death. She wanted to make sure her children got the most out of what she had to leave them.

As a result, I met with Kay and her son and shared with them a strategy I'd used with other clients that had similar wishes. First, we had the trust purchase life insurance on Kay. Second, we took advantage of Kay's advanced age and had the trust purchase an immediate annuity with a portion of the assets. The annuity was able to pay the trust a substantially higher annual payment than if we had invested the money, and it came without any risk. We used those payments to purchase the life insurance and to pay future premiums. In essence, we took a million-dollar trust and turned it into a trust worth three million dollars. This money was guaranteed, which pleased Kay.

Six months before the stock market's roller coaster ride in the fall of 2008, we carved out a portion of the estate and purchased an immediate annuity for Kay. This was done in anticipation of a market downswing (which actually happened). By doing this, we accomplished two things: we were able to cover her core expenses for the rest of her life, and we eliminated the worry about how the stock market was performing. Today, Kay is considering having the trust purchase long-term care insurance for her, which would also protect the legacy she and Don built.

When I present Kay's story to others as an example, I highlight three areas that I believe are critical in developing a successful financial plan:

(1) Use outside money managers to actively manage the money, and not an individual whose time is split between managing money and obtaining new clients. We see this as a conflict of interest and ultimately not in the client's best interest.

(2) Use insurance to leverage the estate and protect it for the heirs. In Kay's case, we had the trust purchase insurance, which maximized the legacy for her children.

(3) Make smart choices to gain peace of mind. By age 80, Kay understood that she needed to continue investing a portion of her assets in the market. However, she also needed assurance that her core expenses would be taken care of, regardless of how the market was performing. By carving out a portion of the estate with an immediate annuity, we could remove the risk and give her peace of mind.

The story of Don and Kay demonstrates the power of planning and, more importantly, the advantage of planning with a team of professionals who collaborate for the benefit of the client. As a financial advisor, my position was to act as Don and Kay's chief financial officer — holding the compass and getting them to their goals.

Nugget of Wisdom

Planning is critical. You need a Primary Financial Coordinator and need to establish a trusted team of professionals that review your overall financial picture — not just their own individual piece.

About the Author

Martin V. Higgins, CFP, is the president of Family Wealth Management, where he oversees and coordinates the finances for a select group of families and businesses in the Delaware Valley. In 2002, Marty was inducted into Research Magazine's Hall of Fame, which annually recognizes the top financial advisors in the United States. His continuous pursuit of education provides him with the knowledge and skills necessary to effectively evaluate each client's financial goals and offer creative strategies to preserve and transfer family wealth.

To obtain a special report on "The 16 Key Questions You Need To Ask a Financial Advisor BEFORE You Hire One," contact Marty at (877) 988-7722 or marty@familywealthadvisory.com.

Martin V. Higgins, CFP
Family Wealth Management
Two Greentree Centre, Suite 300, Marlton, NJ 08053
www.familywealthadvisory.com
marty@familywealthadvisory.com
(877) 988-7722

"I SURE WISH I HAD A FINANCIAL PLAN."

Image Courtesy of CopyBoosters.com

The Power of Estate Planning

By Douglas A. Fendrick, Esquire,
and Jamie Shuster Morgan, Esquire

All of us understand that we *should* have a Will in place, but many do not believe they need a complete "estate plan." That misguided belief, however, has everything to do with not understanding what an "estate plan" is. An "estate plan" incorporates a Will, a Durable General Power of Attorney, a Health Care Power of Attorney and, if appropriate, one or more Trust, in order to help manage a client's affairs both during life and after death. The following paragraphs highlight why everyone should have each such document in place and, therefore, why we all need an "estate plan"—not just a Will.

<u>Why You Need A Will</u>: A Will is a document which becomes effective upon your death. Under the terms of a Will, you

appoint someone (an "Executor") to collect and administer your estate (pay your final debts, expenses and taxes, etc.) and to distribute your assets to designated beneficiaries. If you do not designate an Executor in your Will, one will be appointed after your death, it just may not be someone you'd select for yourself. In a Will, you also specify how your estate is to be distributed. When you do not have a Will, you still have an estate plan. However, that plan is one that is imposed by the State in which you reside (known as the "intestacy" laws). In the absence of a Will, the intestacy laws will govern the distribution of your property. Also, it is important to have a well drafted Will. Poorly drafted Wills include ambiguities and often result in disputes among family members. You can also appoint a Guardian of minor children in a Will. The selection of a Guardian is, perhaps, the most difficult decision for a couple to make. However, failure to designate a Guardian could result in your children being cared for by family members that you would not have selected yourself.

Why You Need A Trust: Trusts take many forms: some are revocable, some are irrevocable, some become effective at death, and others are effective during life. Many people do not believe that their "estate" is large enough to warrant a Trust. Again, however, I believe that this misguided belief has everything to do with not understanding what a Trust can help you accomplish. For example, no matter how large or small your estate, you want to ensure your assets pass to the beneficiaries of your choosing. For many clients, that means to children and ultimately grandchildren. However, if you leave your estate to a child, outright, now that child has control over where those assets will ultimately be distributed. Those inherited assets (which you hope will pass down to grandchildren) could be lost to the child's creditors, the child's former spouse (in divorce) or be bequeathed to someone other than your grandchildren upon the child's death (potentially, passing to a son or daughter-in-law). If, instead, the assets were left ito a Family Protection Trust for the child's lifetime benefit, upon the child's ultimate death, the assets could pass to your grandchildren. Trusts are also helpful vehicles to manage funds until a beneficiary attains an age at which he or she can responsibly manage the funds. When you leave assets to an eighteen year old, you might be thinking College Tuition, but he might be thinking New Car. A Trust can help protect the beneficiary from himself or herself. Finally, of course, Trusts can be used to help minimize, or even eliminate, death taxes. For New Jersey residents, for example, a married couple with assets in excess of $675,000 should have Trusts in their estate planning documents to help reduce, or eliminate, the New Jersey estate tax.

Why You Need A Durable General Power of Attorney: A Durable General Power of Attorney (a "DGPOA") is a document in which you designate someone, an Agent, to assist you manage your affairs during lifetime. A DGPOA ceases to be effective upon your death. Many people operate under the incorrect assumption that, even without a DGPOA, their spouse can handle their financial affairs for them. Marriage does not give your spouse any authority over your finances, even if you are unable to manage your affairs for yourself. Similarly, many young people think that they are too young to need a DGPOA; they think that they are capable of managing their affairs themselves. They may very well be so capable, but in the event they are in an accident or unexpectedly unable to manage their affairs themselves, it is critical that someone be designated to do so. Everyone should have a DGPOA in place, regardless of your familial or financial situation. Failure to have a DGPOA could result in an expensive and time consuming Guardianship proceeding in court to have someone appointed to manage your affairs for you.

Why You Need A Health Care Power Of Attorney: As with a DGPOA, everyone should have a Health Care Power of Attorney ("HCPOA") in place. In a HCPOA, you designate someone as your Health Care Agent to make medical decisions for you in the event you are unable to make them for yourself. A Health Care Agent is empowered to talk with your doctors, access your medical records and authorize consent to treatment. A Health Care Agent can also be empowered to make ultimate decisions regarding the removal or refusal of life support or life sustaining measures. With respect to end-of-life decisions, talking with your Health Care Agent about your wishes is as important as the document itself. You need to be certain that your Health Care Agent understands your wishes and can carry them out.

Why You Need An Estate Plan: Each of the documents highlighted above serve an independent function in the administration of your affairs. Just because you designate an Executor under your Will does not mean that your Executor has any power at all during your lifetime. It is imperative that each one of us sit down with an estate planning attorney to discuss our desires and intentions, as well as our financial situation, to ensure that we have the proper plan—the proper ***estate plan***—in place to carry out those intentions, both during and after life.

About the Authors

Douglas A. Fendrick, Esquire, and Jamie Shuster Morgan, Esquire, of the Law Offices of Douglas A. Fendrick, located in Voorhees, NJ, practice exclusively in the areas of estate planning, estate administration and elder law. Doug and Jamie are both admitted to practice law in New Jersey and Pennsylvania, and Doug is also admitted to practice before the United States Tax Court. Doug and Jamie are both frequent lectures on areas of estate planning, estate administration and elder law. Doug earned his B.S., cum laude, from Rider University, his J.D. Degree from Rutgers University School of Law, and his LL.M. in Taxation from Temple University. Jamie earned her B.A. from Pennsylvania State University, her J.D. Degree from Rutgers University

School of Law, and her LL.M. in Taxation from New York University. Doug is a Certified Elder Law Attorney through the National Elder Law Foundation, an Accredited Estate Planning Specialist through the American Bar Association and a Certified Public Accountant. They can be reached through their website: www.fendricklaw.com, or by calling (856) 489-8388.

Where Will Your Money Go? It's Your Choice

By Jay Van Beusekom, RHU, LUTCF, IAR

Do you know the number one reason senior citizens run out of money? It's not from living too long, and it's not from bad investments. The primary cause of financial devastation among senior citizens is the catastrophic cost of long-term medical care. Health care costs are rising every year, and very few of us have the assets to pay outright for the care we may need. However, this type of coverage is often the last consideration on a long list of places people's money must go when they come to me to plan for retirement. My experience is that many times it's not even on the list at all.

I met Dave and Helen back in February of 2002. They had owned and operated their family business for many years, and

Dave was fast approaching his retirement age of 65, with Helen soon to follow. My property and casualty agent referred them to me because my specialty is working with retirees and pre-retirees in all aspects of their financial planning. I focus not only on long-term planning to make sure my clients can enjoy their retirement years with financial security, but also on their investments intended for their children.

Dave and Helen were ideal candidates for me because their business was truly their greatest asset, and they were not certain how to protect all they had worked for up to this point. Like many people I encounter, Dave and Helen hadn't considered the 'unexpected' aspects of retirement planning, namely the need for long-term care insurance.

They had addressed some health care issues, allowing for Medicare supplement planning, but they had never considered long-term care expenses. Initially, like many people do, they had some reservations about investing in another insurance premium. They assumed their current assets would be enough to cover any such expenses, or that they were not at high risk for needing such care.

Both Dave and Helen were shocked to learn that after a couple reaches age 65, there's a greater than 70% chance that one or both of them will require some form of long-term care in their lifetime. Whether it's home care, assisted living, or a nursing home, people always think it's going to happen to 'someone else.' The fact is statistics paint a very different picture.

The other sobering fact, is that your money is going to one of a few different places, either to taxes, your kids, a charity, or a nursing home. Obviously, most people want the majority of their money to go to their children and their favorite charities; taxes and nursing homes are usually not their first choices.

After I educated them further about those statistics and illustrated just how much they had at risk, Dave and Helen were ready to move forward. Within about six months we were able to issue a policy on Helen. Dave wasn't immediately eligible because he had some recent health problems, but all of that was soon resolved and he was fully covered a few, short months later.

Just about two years into their coverage, Helen was hospitalized for an inter-cranial hemorrhage. Within weeks she was admitted to a nursing home for extended care and rehabilitation. Fortunately, this was a temporary state of affairs and she recovered and came home, but it was the beginning of a series of health issues for her. Earlier this year, she fell at home due to some lingering effects of her brain hemorrhage, and once again required temporary nursing home care.

Because of their extensive long-term care insurance coverage, Helen was able to utilize a home health care aide for some time, and remain in their home while she recovered further. Her health has fluctuated over the years, and she is now in an assisted-living apartment complex where she can get 24-hour care and assistance with her medication and meals. Dave is able to bring her home from time to time, using a home health care aide when needed. They can also spend time together in Door County, which is in northern Wisconsin.

The result is that Dave and Helen are still able to do many of the things they want to do, choose the type of care they want, and where they want it. That's what this long-term care has been able to do for them. As important as it is to protect and preserve your assets, it is just as important to provide peace of mind for your spouse, children, and family.

Dave does not have to worry about the quality of Helen's care. He knows she is in a comfortable and reputable facility, and he and his family are in control of the decisions that affect her life. He knows that the burden of her daily care does not fall solely onto his shoulders, nor to their children. Furthermore, he knows that if his health suffers, he will be cared for in the same manner. All of this is a great relief to Dave and Helen, and they can still leave a legacy for their children and grandchildren.

Had Dave and Helen foregone long-term care insurance, their life would be vastly different. Eventually, they would have had to start spending down their retirement nest egg. This would have been especially painful for them, as their 'nest egg' was actually the family business they nurtured for many years. They sold the business just last year, knowing that the proceeds were theirs to live on now and distribute to their children in the future. It would have broken their hearts to see that money funneled into nursing homes and care facilities instead.

In Helen's case, her health challenges have been ongoing, so the drain on their finances would have continued for an extended period. The way things look for her now, she will likely never be able to live without some form of medical assistance, and she can take comfort in the fact that her care won't impact her husband's or her children's future.

Even with the sobering statistics and compelling real-life stories such as this, I still have clients who are reluctant to consider long-term care insurance. I explain to them that what they are really doing by purchasing that coverage is protecting themselves. In the simplest terms, I refer to it as the "ABC's" of long-term care: "A" stands for your assets. First and foremost people need to make sure that their assets are protected for themselves, their spouse, and their children or favorite charity. "B" stands for not being a burden to your family. They are going to want to help you, but very few families are equipped to handle the demands of full-time care. Besides, everyone wants to preserve their dignity, and most people prefer a health care professional to assist them with bathing, feeding, and dressing themselves, not leaving that to their children. Finally, the "C" stands for choice of care. Being able to choose the type of care you want, and where you want to receive it. If given the option, most people would prefer to stay at home rather than be forced into a nursing home or assisted living facility.

I understand my clients' concerns about the cost of this extra coverage, but I explain that they truly cannot afford to be without it. The cost of health care is going to keep going up every year, at least by 5%. For that reason, I urge clients to include inflation protection on their policies so their coverage keeps up with the risings costs and doesn't become obsolete by the time they need to use it. I cannot stress enough with my clients, that the odds are very high that they or their spouse will likely require such care at some point in their lives. People always think it's going to happen to someone else, and sadly, that is usually not the case.

Given this set of circumstances, I still recognize that every client's situation is different, and I take great pains to tailor the coverage to best suit them and their families. I look at what kind of monthly income streams they have coming in, and if they are using all of it that for living expenses. We then determine what portion of the unused income, if they have any, could be set aside each month specifically for long-term care expenses. Investment assets are considered as well, and in some cases they can be utilized to generate income for cost of care, without impacting their current living 'allowance'. It may seem daunting, but that is why planning with an experienced professional is so important.

The bottom line is, without prudent long-term care planning, you are putting your future at risk and potentially causing great hardship for your spouse and children. The right choices can make all the difference in the world.

Nugget of Wisdom

When people are doing long-term care planning, they're protecting their assets for the lifestyle they've saved for their whole lives. Proper planning gives you peace of mind, knowing that when something happens — not *if*, but *when* — you and your family will be okay.

About the Author

Jay Van Beusekom is the founder and president of Jay Van Beusekom Financial Advisor LLC, a full-service financial solutions company. Jay has been helping pre-retirees and retirees in southeastern Wisconsin since 1985, and is committed to ensuring that his clients both meet their retirement goals and enjoy comfortable retirement years.

Contact Jay for a special report, "Long-Term Care, Is it Right for You?" and mention this book, Promises Kept, to receive a complimentary, in-depth consultation about your options for long-term care planning. Jay can be reached at (414) 359-1756, via e-mail at jay.vanbeusekom@adviserfocus.com, or you may visit his company website, www.why-jay.com, for further information.

Jay Van Beusekom, RHU, LUTCF, IAR

Jay Van Beusekom Financial Advisor LLC

www.why-jay.com

jay.vanbeusekom@adviserfocus.com

(414) 359-1756

"PAYING YOURSELF FIRST HAS REALLY PAID OFF FOR YOU!"

Image Courtesy of CopyBoosters.com

Building From the Ground Up

By Michael G. Herman, ChFC

I look at my career as a financial advisor as akin to that of a construction business owner. I'm helping people to build their dreams and lay the foundation for their lives. One of my greatest challenges is finding the right products and services for each client. I don't just run down a list of products and plug in my client's name. That would be like a physician prescribing the same drug to each patient without taking x-rays or looking inside, focusing only on the superficial.

I pride myself on getting to know my clients first and establishing a relationship with them before I determine their needs. I allow them to describe to me their goals and dreams for the future, and then we can work together to achieve them. The other component, though, is planning for the unexpected, which many people are reluctant to do. Your life can change in an instant, and I want my clients to be prepared for that.

Such was the case with a young married couple, Tom and Maria. I was introduced to them through Tom's father, Barry, who owned a small construction company which employed Tom and his brother Andy. I had done business planning for Barry, advising him on life insurance and disability coverage, and had established a very good relationship with him.

Tom and Maria were just a few years younger than I, so we had a lot in common and could relate well to one another. They were just getting their lives started and had bought a new home, so we started with the groundwork, what I call 'the foundation planning'. I advised them to secure coverage on their home, their income, life insurance, and also set up a savings plan for the future.

One aspect that I stressed to this young couple was disability insurance, which would provide coverage if either one was injured or disabled in some way that they could no longer work, even for a short period of time.

As is common with a lot of my clients, Tom and Maria were resistant at first, thinking that they were too young and healthy to worry about such things. Tom had a good job with his father's construction company and Maria worked for a high-end beauty salon in town. They were vivacious and active, living the good life. Both were enjoying their home and the pleasures their steady incomes afforded them such as traveling, water skiing, and other activities. Children were in their immediate future, and they could not have been more excited about what lay ahead for them.

It is my responsibility to urge my clients to plan for the unexpected twists and turns that life can hold for us. Tom was especially hard to convince on that issue, saying "Ah, you know, Mike, I'm young and I'm only making $2,500 to $3,000 a month in this construction business and I mean, it's good money, but …", he paused. "I don't think anything's going to happen to me."

A few years later, Tom was at work with his father and brother, building a custom home. They were putting up a large side wall, and Tom thought that it was secured as he turned to walk away. The other workers let go of the wall piece and it came crashing down on top of Tom, breaking his neck and instantly paralyzing him from the neck down. Tom was just 35 years old.

Barry called me with the shocking news, and at that point, Tom was in the hospital on a breathing tube, fighting for his life. He survived, thanks to his robust physical health, and the long process towards recovery and rehabilitation began. Of course, Tom was unable to work, and though they had very good health insurance, a sizable share of medical bills loomed over them.

After Tom was home, I met with him to tackle the medical bills. Not even a few minutes into our discussion, Tom stopped, looked at me, and said, "Mike, I gotta tell you. I can't thank you enough for pushing me to get the disability insurance." The coverage was allowing Tom and Maria to stay in their home and focus on his care and well-being. "You don't know what this is gonna mean to us," Tom said. "I may not have thought my income was a lot, but now that I know I'm not gonna get it…." His voice trailed off, too choked up to speak. It was emotional; we were both tearing up.

Fortunately, Tom had excellent health coverage that gave his family the option of sending him to some of the more advanced therapy centers in Colorado to continue his care. Over a period of about a year and a half, Tom's outlook improved and therapists were able to regain movement in the upper part of his body, though he was still confined to a wheelchair.

Tom and Maria did not anticipate the next challenge facing them — Tom was denied Social Security disability benefits. Since he could use his arms and had suffered no brain damage, Tom was still considered employable as a telemarketer, and therefore ineligible for benefits. If not for their existing disability insurance and Maria's considerable salary, they would have been in danger of losing their home and significantly lowering their quality of life.

The challenges were many for this young couple. Maria was managing to keep her very good job at the beauty salon, and her income of $80,000-$90,000 was a welcome relief when paired with their disability benefits. But Maria was tackling Tom's therapy appointments herself; she spent many hours each week taking him to and from therapies, some lasting two to three hours, and it began to take a toll on her job performance.

Unfortunately, Maria's employer was growing increasingly frustrated with her frequent absences and suddenly fired her. Not only did she lose a healthy income, she also lost out on the potential partnership she was working towards with the salon, further impacting their future. Once again, their disability coverage saved the day. Along with that income and some help from their parents, Tom and Maria had enough money to stay afloat.

Tom's accident changed every aspect of their lives. Their plans for children changed, as now their lives revolved around Tom's care and recovery, and Maria getting her career back on its feet. They had to renovate their home to accommodate Tom's needs and allow him some more independence, which made it possible for Maria to go back to work. Tom and Maria came through this struggle with their marriage intact and have accepted the life-altering changes that came along in an instant. Tom has gotten some feeling back in his right leg and actually can walk with a quad cane, though he still struggles with physical pain and nerve damage. Maria has now opened up her own beauty salon, realizing a dream of her own, and the bonus is that Tom is able to work part time in Maria's salon, selling and marketing her products via Internet sales. He goes in two to three days a week, and now they work together to build their business as a family, giving Tom a renewed sense of purpose.

The picture for Tom and Maria would have been vastly different had they not had disability coverage. For many of us, the reality is if we miss a few paychecks, we can quickly be in serious trouble. Add to that the rising costs of medical care and home health aides, and it's almost untenable for most people.

I think the younger we are, the less we are inclined to consider disability coverage. I ask people what their most important financial asset is and they usually say their house, but in reality it is their income, their ability to get up every morning and go to work and provide for their families. People need to consider that no matter what age they are, anybody can become disabled. It could be a car accident, a chronic disease, a workplace injury. Anything can happen to you without warning.

I certainly can't prevent bad things from happening to my clients, but what I can do is provide them with my knowledge, present them with the facts, and urge them not to live in denial. The reality is, you have a one out of four chance of having a disability lasting longer than five years. I wouldn't bet against those odds, would you? My philosophy is this with my clients: whatever happens to you in life has to do with how prepared you are to deal with it. If you are not prepared, I can guarantee it's going to be a lot worse.

Nugget of Wisdom

What would your life look like today without an income? Take responsible action to protect your family's most important asset — your income.

About the Author

Michael G. Herman, ChFC is the president of Golden Wealth Solutions, Inc. a full-service financial advising company that provides a financial foundation for families to build on during their changing lives. Mike is committed to customer service and shares his company's value statement: "At Golden Wealth Solutions we are concerned about you, your values, and your goals in life. We want you to experience the value of having a long-term relationship with a trusted advisor."

To contact Mike for a financial check-up, an engaged review of your current financial situation, call (303) 456-1913; or e-mail him at mike.gws@adviserfocus.com or visit his company website at www.goldenwealthsolutions.com for more information.

Michael G. Herman, ChFC

Financial Advisor

Golden Wealth Solutions, Inc.

www.goldenwealthsolutions.com

mike.gws@adviserfocus.com

(303) 456-1913

A REGULAR FINANCIAL CHECK-UP IS AS IMPORTANT AS A MEDICAL CHECK-UP.

Image Courtesy of CopyBoosters.com

Preservation of Wealth Through Trusts

By Anthony G. Engrassia, ChFC

One of the most difficult issues of the financial planning process is how to disperse funds once you are no longer living. My clients have worked hard during their lives to build wealth. They are, like most people, emotionally tied to the substantial efforts that went into building their riches. For them, it's most important to preserve the funds for their loved ones and not watch their hard-earned money be absorbed by taxes. Many also seek to donate a portion of their net worth to charities.

As I help clients through this process, one issue I face continually is trying to figure out what the financial needs of their loved ones will be once they are gone.

What makes my clients wealthy is they haven't spent unnecessarily throughout their lifetime; instead they have chosen to save their earnings. This habit usually forms during the early years of their marriage. They understand the value of a dollar and perhaps have even seen "good fortune" quickly disappear, forcing them to start all over again. Over time, meager savings grow and many are able to make wise investments along the way.

Because of their sound financial habits to save, some of my clients have foregone the flash and flamboyance of shiny new vehicles in the driveway or beautiful jewels around their neck. For many years, they simply weren't willing to part with their money. They may now drive a shimmering high performance car and have a few more pearls in their collection, but those luxuries came after years of sacrifice. This isn't always the case with their children.

Their children grew up in a different time, with privileges their parents didn't have. This is natural, as it is every parent's wish to provide their children with more than they had growing up. Often parents are concerned about how to properly disperse their wealth — in the best interests of their heirs and for tax considerations.

Setting up a trust, a financial tool I regularly recommend, can speak for the parents by carrying out their wishes, when they are gone.

When the parents are planning their estates, they don't always trust their children to be responsible and wise with their newfound inheritance. They often view their children as "spendthrifty" and are fearful that their hard-earned money will be spent on frivolous and lavish purchases. Establishing a trust that pays out a regular stream of "income" can prevent this scenario from ever happening.

Many of my clients grow fearful when they look into the future, to a time when their children become their age. They trust their children to be responsible with their inheritance, but also want to ensure their money is preserved for their grandkids. They wonder what would happen to the family wealth should one of their married children die. They love their daughters-in-law and sons-in-law, but if something should happen to one of their own children, other issues and scenarios may arise. For example, what if the son-in-law or daughter-in-law remarries? Would the money become co-mingled with this union and leave less for the grandchildren? A trust addresses these issues and keeps the money separate by earmarking it specifically for the children, grandchildren and subsequent generations.

Finally, I have clients who worry that an inheritance will "ruin" their children. This is a valid concern —I've seen time and time again where honest, hard-working people win the lottery and their lives become corrupt because they aren't equipped to handle their newfound wealth. Establishing a trust eliminates this concern. A trust can be used as a source of income for children, giving additional enjoyment throughout their lifetime, instead of all at once.

How does a trust work? It's a common question and I answer it the following way: A trust is intended to speak for you after you are gone. A trust carries out your wishes. You can generally establish whatever parameters you'd like within your trust. You can allow your children to have an income; you can have the money used for health, maintenance, or support purposes. You can pay for your grandchildren's college education from the trust. You can even arrange to give your loved ones a lump-sum amount during special times in their lives, like graduation from college, marriage, or the birth of a great-grandchild. A trust allows you to decide.

One of the first steps in setting up a trust is deciding on a trustee — the person who carries out the trust grantor's intent. Many times the first instinct of my clients is to choose a family member, perhaps one of the kids or another sibling. I discourage this practice and usually recommend using an outside trust company to carry out a client's wishes. Here's why: When a family member is the trustee, it is his or her job to carry out your wishes as expressed by the terms of the trust. This means that not only do they need the time and experience to administer the trusts, but they are also are now burdened with possibly saying "no" to loved ones seeking money. Sometimes the "no" is taken so personally that feelings are impossible to overcome, causing discontent within the family for years - possibly the remainder of their lives. By hiring a trust company, you ensure this will never happen.

Years ago, third parties who handled trusts earned a bad reputation, and rightly so. Back then and in some cases still, banks also had a hand in the investment side of the trust. This was a conflict of interest, with the banks not wanting to relinquish funds to the family members based on the bank's own vested interests. Rest assured, this rarely happens anymore, and my advice is to hire a trust company whose only job is to carry out your wishes, while I focus on what I do best – growing and protecting your family's wealth.

Hiring a trust company isn't free. The fee for carrying out your wishes as laid out in the administrative provisions of your trust is usually a percentage of the trust which is paid by the trust once you have passed — so your children are not burdened with this expense. For this fee, the trust company will administer the trust based on the provisions, perform all of the income and principal distributions, prepare quarterly principal and income reports, perform the trust tax remittance and tax reporting, and handle the filing and payment of the trust's tax liabilities to the IRS.

Before my clients set up a trust through an attorney, I help them answer many questions — often hard questions — so they know precisely how they want their wealth to be distributed. Some questions that need answers include: Do you want your children to get an annual income and/or a lump-sum when they reach a certain age? Do you want your children to have access to the principal in certain circumstances, or do you want the principal to stay intact? How many generations would they like this trust to last? And do they want the parents of future generations determining how and when children receive money, or do they want to determine that?

It takes time to determine what choices are best for you. However, one of the immediate benefits clients experience from establishing a trust is the knowledge and peace of mind that their money will be going to the things that enriched their lives the most — their children, their charitable causes, and their community.

The final step I take with my trust clients is to arrange a family meeting between the parents and children. The purpose is not to discuss the amount of money in the trust; instead, the parents share their thoughts and benefits of creating a trust. This helps alleviate any shock or hurt feelings once the parents pass away. The children see that a trust is in place to preserve hard-earned money for future generations … for that truly is the greatest benefit of establishing a trust — preservation of family wealth for generations to come.

Nugget of Wisdom

"We make a living by what we get.

But we make a life by what we give."

—*Winston Churchill*

About the Author

Anthony Engrassia, ChFC, is a founding member of Wealth Management Strategies, Inc., a financial planning and wealth management firm serving Rocky Mount, NC, and surrounding areas. The creator of the Strategic Freedom Process™, he offers clientele a step-by-step process that enables them to enjoy greater personal financial opportunities during their retirement years.

For a no-obligation, complimentary "starter session" consultation to assess your current situation and clarify your personal and financial goals, log onto www.strategicfreedom.com or call (800) 256-7041.

To receive a copy of The Ultimate Gift, the best-selling novel by Jim Stovall, contact Tony at (800) 256-7041 or tony.wmsnc@adviserfocus.com.

Anthony G. Engrassia

Wealth Management Strategies

tony.wmsnc@adviserfocus.com

(800) 256-7041

To learn more about Wealth Management Strategies, read Chapter 7 by Kevin Swan.

"IT'S CALLED INFLATION, SIR."

Image Courtesy of CopyBoosters.com

The Cost of a Zero

By Danny Smith

When I pulled out of the office parking lot on that sunny May morning, all seemed right in the world. Our second child had recently been born, after two years in the business my insurance career was beginning to blossom, and the bills were getting paid on time. Little did I know that within the hour, I would experience a career-defining event that would shock me into a completely different mindset.

The day before, my manager had called me into his office and explained that a policy owner had recently died. He thought it would be a good experience for me to deliver the life insurance check to his widow. I hadn't written the policy, and I didn't know anything about the client. All I knew was this was going to be my first death claim check I'd even delivered.

Although the name on the check didn't tell me how old the person was, I naturally assumed the widow would be older – in her 70s or 80s.

But when I got to the house, what I found was completely different than what I was expecting. The house was a modest one-story home in a nice neighborhood, and there were two little kids' bikes in the front yard along with other toys that kids would play with.

As I walked up to the house, I couldn't help noticing the many leisure-life belongings in the garage. There was a shiny new sports car, what appeared to be new golf clubs, and lots and lots of other grown-up "toys." So it didn't take me long to figure out that delivering this check wouldn't be anything like what I thought. This was a young family.

I knocked at the door and the woman who came to the door was in her late 20s, maybe early 30s, with a little girl beside her who couldn't have been more than four years old. The woman invited me in and said, "Why don't you sit on the couch for a moment, while I finish something up," which I did.

The little girl stayed in the room, and within a minute or two, she was next to me with her doll. Having noticed two bikes in the front yard, I asked if she had any brothers or sisters, and she replied that she had a brother in the first grade. I played with the girl until the mom came in and sat beside me.

I handed her the death claim check for $25,000. As she took the check out of the envelope and looked at it, there was a moment of poignant silence. Then she looked up at me and handed the check back to me. She said, "You might as well take this check back with you. It's not enough to help." I was taken aback, dumbfounded, and didn't know what to do. I also didn't know what to say, so I said the first thing that came to mind, "I'm very sorry, ma'am."

She said, "Danny, it's too late for the 'I'm sorry's.' Look around. He spent money on cars and on stereos; he just bought a new set of golf clubs. If he would've done what the previous agent who sold him the policy recommended and spent a few more dollars, I wouldn't be in this situation." The calmness originally in her voice disappeared and was replaced by anger – anger at her husband for leaving her 'high and dry'.

With my heart pounding, I placed the check on the coffee table. Grasping for words I looked up and asked if there was anything else I could do. With tears trickling down her face she said, "I'm going to lose this house, Danny. There's no way I can keep the house and the cars. All he left me are the kids and a pile of bills. I don't know what I'm going to do."

Her late husband had had a good job, so they were living up to their income level. However, when that ends abruptly, as it did in this case, the little bit that she might've received from Social Security would never take the place of that income, and she realized that.

Feeling that there was nothing else I could do for her, I got up to leave, and as she and the little girl accompanied me to the door, I muttered out a pitiful, "Good luck."

As I backed out of the driveway, I saw the little girl in the doorway, waving goodbye to me. As I waived back, I doubt she saw the tears in my eyes or felt my heavy heart. Driving away I thought, "The check was for $25,000. If there was one more zero on that check, just one more zero, she would've been okay. It wouldn't have replaced her husband, but just one more zero would've turned it into a $250,000 check."

As I drove down the road I realized just how closely this family mirrored my own. My wife and I had two young kids, a house, and two cars – just like the family I'd just visited. I also thought about how my own father died suddenly when I was only five years old leaving my mom with her three sons to fend for ourselves. And just like the husband of the widow I'd just visited, he died without enough life insurance. For another $25 or $30 a month, her husband could have added a zero to that check.

I drove past the house a few months later, and it was empty. The 'For Sale' sign was still there, but the family had moved away. I never did learn what happened to that family. After 26 years, I still think about that woman and her daughter.

How much does one more zero cost in life when you're trying to do the right thing and provide insurance?

Mutual of Omaha taught me how to sell their product. I knew how to sell insurance, but nobody had ever taught me how to deliver a death claim check when it's an inadequate amount. What type of a rehearsal could you have for something like that? Ever since then, I've kept that story in my heart, and tried to convey that message to my clients.

I hope that in my career the claim checks I've delivered since then have been for whatever the right amount is or even above the right amount, because that story has always stayed within me.

If the husband added just another dollar a day, he could have changed everything in his family's life.

If your home was worth $250,000, you wouldn't insure it for $25,000, would you? The husband chose to insure his life nowhere near what its value was.

So to younger couples, I have often said, "Here's the cost of a zero and the price you pay for not paying that small extra cost for that extra zero on the check," because with insurance, it's better to have too much than too little.

The focus of my practice now is retirement planning, although I work with clients of all ages. Using our unique Asset Harvester Process helps you determine your dreams and objectives, and then we can provide a personal solution to a financially secure future. We empower people to focus on the real wealth in their lives. It gives our clients a feeling of comfort knowing that by taking action, they've removed the stress and complexity from their retirement years.

More often than not, we've found that insurance and financial products are purchased on an incremental basis without regard to a long-term planning strategy. Our process allows us to assist our clients in designing a personal retirement roadmap. We are a relationship-driven financial services firm; it's a partnership between the client and me.

When I first meet with a potential client, we go through a Discovery Session. It's a chance for us to get to know each other and decide if it makes sense to move forward together. Do we get along? Will we work well together? All of this is important in the relationship.

It's also important when you're planning for your retirement that you find a professional that can understand and incorporate everything that is important to you, including finances and personal goals. You need a strategy to address your entire future, not just one aspect of it.

My objective with each client is to make sure that the product or service I recommend meets their objectives. I often think about that widow and how different her life might have been if her husband had just realized the importance of having the right amount of life insurance. I put myself in my clients' shoes, knowing that they've put their trust in me to guide them.

Nugget of Wisdom

There is no way of knowing what dangers lay ahead in your future, but you can plan for the possibilities. Life insurance is the only financial product available with a 100 percent guarantee that the "right amount" of zeros will be on the check. How many zeros do you need?

About the Author

Danny Smith is founder of Daniels Financial Group, a relationship-driven financial services firm dedicated to providing clients with needs-based solutions to their long-term financial services objectives. The firm's motto – Quality Planning for a Quality Life℠ – is based on their unique ability to" take the complexity out of the plan" and our stringent commitment to the highest quality products and services. To meet with Danny and schedule a Discovery Session℠, please contact him at his Lorain, Ohio, office by calling (440) 277-7676 or (800) 783-2061. You can also email him at danny.dfg@adviserfocus.com or visit his website at www.danielsfinancialgroup.com.

Danny Smith

Daniels Financial Group, Inc.

www.danielsfinancialgroup.com

danny.dfg@adviserfocus.com

(440) 277-7676

(800) 783-2061

"I WOULDN'T HAVE THESE BILLS IF DON WOULD'VE BOUGHT THAT LIFE INSURANCE POLICY."

Image Courtesy of CopyBoosters.com

A Financially Free Future

By Kevin J. Swan, ChFC, CASL

Margie was in her mid-50s when her husband of 20 years, who had handled all the family's money issues, died of cancer. Unfortunately, he, like many financial managers of households, hadn't pragmatically prepared for the worst-case scenario. He didn't have a will. He didn't have nearly enough life insurance. And he hadn't ever brought Margie into the financial process. It's a commonplace occurrence, especially in "Baby Boomers," but it's distressing to see nonetheless.

I have been in the financial business for a long time, so when Margie was referred to me by a family friend, I wasn't surprised to learn that she hadn't been involved in the financial aspects of her marriage. But that knowledge didn't make her story any less poignant.

After her husband passed away, Margie wanted to grieve but was left with the reality that she had to get her finances in order immediately. This left her in a truly difficult situation — she desperately needed to take time for herself, but had to handle a financial crisis instead.

She was riddled with conflicting thoughts. Would she need to get a job? Should she start volunteering? Did she need to be in Florida with her daughters? Did she need to be in Ohio with her parents? She was very religious and looked to God to provide guidance, but that didn't change the fact that she was more than a little scared.

As we began looking over Margie's financial situation, it became apparent that financial planning had not been a priority in her household. Many of the items Margie and her husband owned were only in his name. Other items were in both their names. It was a very complex situation. And she was alone.

Because I consider myself to be a financial partner with my clients, I was very frank with Margie. When she asked, "What do I need to do?", I responded honestly. I told her we needed to take inventory of her assets to start a process that would ensure she had enough money and stability for the rest of her life. I also assured her that I would help her every step of the way.

Through my experiences, I have learned that complicated cases like Margie's are best solved by a team. So I called two professionals with whom I have strategic alliances — an attorney and a CPA. Together, we made trips to the courthouse to go through the probate process to rectify the "no will" situation. During our trips, we also addressed the fact that some of the vehicles were only in Margie's husband's name.

During the time we were engaged in the probate process, Margie and I created a timeline of what needed to be accomplished … and by when. Obviously, she needed to be able to pay her immediate bills, so our first order of business was to guarantee that she had enough money in a readily accessible savings account.

Next on our agenda, we examined her stock options and the life insurance monies. We had to tackle some tough question. Would she move to be closer to her kids? Would she stay in the area and get a job? It involved a great deal of soul-searching; Margie had never imagined life without her husband. Now, she was forced to plan for an unexpected future.

One of Margie's chief desires was to not repeat the same fiscal mistakes again, so we created a complete estate plan, a will, and a health care power of attorney. Now, her daughters will always be on the same page as she is and be aware of her final wishes.

One of the biggest concerns for Margie was guaranteeing that she would be financially secure for the rest of her life. So I suggested that Margie allow me to help her create "buckets" of money for her to live off.

The "Bucket Theory" tool, as I call it, ensures that she is going to get money to pay her bills. Essentially, we put monies in different "buckets" and we'll "harvest" those buckets over the course of Margie's lifetime. We've ensured that money will always be available for her no matter what happens to the market.

Consequently, Margie has a monthly in-flow of cash and she's now living a comfortable lifestyle without having to work. She's been able to spend more time with her daughters, her parents, and her sisters.

Best of all, Margie is now able to mourn for her husband. She's financially secure, and that's given her the opportunity to freely explore her new role, not to mention focus her energies on doting over her first grandchild!

There are many things that Margie and her husband could have done differently. Would it have been pragmatic if they had engaged in estate planning? Absolutely. Margie could have avoided attorney's costs in the probate process. Should her husband have purchased more life insurance protection? There's no doubt that would have helped keep Margie set financially. But they never talked about it and ran out of time.

That's why my mantra to clients is to keep the lines of communication open when it comes to being fiscally responsible. Too many husbands and wives put off planning until it's too late. Or one spouse assumes that the other spouse has done everything, then finds out he or she hasn't.

To help alleviate and solve these common problems for my clients, I've helped develop and trademark a process for people who want to take charge of their financial futures.

Our company, Wealth Management Strategies, has a step-by-step method called "The Strategic Freedom Process™." It's a planning process I've found to be extremely effective for clients of all ages, but especially for those who are entering their retirement years.

Part of the model deals with what I call a "procrastination trap," which occurs out of benign neglect. Couples live their lives and spend their money … today. They don't worry too much about tomorrow, figuring they'll do that some other time. They assume there will always be more time to write down the plans they have "in their heads," but that never happens. In the meantime, those couples wind up paying unnecessary taxes, having poor allocation of their savings, and not assigning beneficiaries.

Whenever I talk with clients, I inevitably have someone who tells me that they didn't realize they had fallen into a "procrastination trap." My bringing it up triggers a realization that something needs to be done.

Margie's story illustrates what I see over and over again — people become unable to enjoy their retirement to the fullest. When a man or woman passes away before planning financially for his or her spouse, the surviving family member can be left with a substantially different retirement than he or she intended.

Not surprisingly, individuals often are unable to fulfill their personal and financial goals, even if they have the money to make those goals a reality! That's why I always recommend writing down some financial goals to share with loved ones and, eventually, a financial planner.

The Strategic Freedom Process™ essentially involves working as a team. I and my colleagues have developed strategies so clientele can benefit from greater personal and financial opportunities during their retirement years. In layman's terms, my clients know that they won't "out-live" their money.

Financial freedom isn't about investing in products, because anyone can play the stock market, anyone can hire a stockbroker. But the Strategic Freedom Process™ offers an experience akin to having a personal CFO. I not only help clients put financial strategies down on paper, but I also help to bring those plans to fruition. Of course, every family has intrinsic values; consequently, the Strategic Freedom Process™ has been established to work with those values.

It's always fascinating for me to help clients answer unasked questions, such as "Are we paying too much in taxes?", "Do we have the proper beneficiaries designated on our accounts?" and "Is there a better way of transferring this wealth to our kids without paying taxes?" The Strategic Freedom Process™ outlines ideas to help clients change and enhance their financial situations.

Written financial plans and written financial strategies are amazingly powerful, as Margie now tells her friends and family members. On paper, you can flesh them out and determine if you have the resources and tools to achieve them.

Individuals should enjoy their retirement and live purposefully, not fearfully. By writing everything down, they know ahead of time what opportunities await them.

Nugget of Wisdom

If there's one piece of advice I have for people, it's to not only have a plan, but make sure to write it down. Have a strategy to transfer your wealth and knowledge in a way that reflects your values.

Brian Tracey, acclaimed entrepreneur, noted: "There's never enough time to do everything, but there is always enough time to do the most important thing." To me, that says it all. You're not going to be able to accomplish everything at one time, but you can and should take care of the important things.

About the Author

Kevin J. Swan is a partner with Wealth Management Strategies. A co-creator of the Strategic Freedom Process™, he offers clientele a step-by-step process that enables them to enjoy greater personal financial opportunities during their retirement years. For a special Wealth Management Strategies report, "The Costly Mistakes that Retirees Make and Simple Ways to Avoid Them," and a no-obligation, complimentary "starter session" consultation to assess your current situation and clarify your personal and financial goals, log onto www.strategicfreedom.com or call (800) 256-7041.

Kevin J. Swan
Wealth Management Strategies
www.strategicfreedom.com
Kevin.wmsnc@adviserforcus.com
(919) 792-1830
(800) 256-7041

To learn more about Wealth Management Strategies, read Chapter Five by Anthony Engrassia.

"EXCUSE ME LADIES, I NEED TO TAKE THIS CALL FROM MY FINANCIAL ADVISOR."

Image Courtesy of CopyBoosters.com

Risky Business: Do Not Gamble with Your Future

By Dana F. Troske

You might be surprised at how many people in this country have a gambling problem. No, I am not talking about frittering away their money at casinos or poker tournaments, or betting on football. I am talking about people gambling on their very future — their financial stability, their peace of mind, their legacy for their children — because they do not think it is worth the risk. Yet these same people will buy lottery tickets, knowing full well they have less than a 'one in a million' chance of winning anything.

What if I told you that you have a one in two chance of requiring long-term care of at least ninety days once you reach age 65? Sometimes it takes another person's misfortune to convince people it's time to confront this issue head-on.

Richard and Beverly were referred to me by another client of mine. They were getting ready to retire and were encouraged to put things in order after seeing some friends of theirs suffer debilitating illnesses — stroke, Alzheimer's disease — and spend considerable time in nursing homes. The couple saw their assets drained very quickly, and Richard and Beverly wanted to avoid that situation at all costs. In that respect, they did not need much convincing to purchase a Long-Term Care Insurance policy.

At the time I consulted them, Richard was 61 and Beverly was 60, with both enjoying relatively good health. I figured out the most comprehensive policy for their financial situation and lifestyle, and they felt comfortable that their assets were both protected for the present and preserved for their children.

About one year into their contract, I spent some time with Richard and Beverly at a charity golf tournament that I organized. Richard was an avid golfer and I invited him to play and bring Beverly to enjoy the day. Right away I noticed she was not herself. She would just get out of the golf cart and wander off, and Richard would have to chase after her and bring her back. "What is wrong with Beverly?" I asked. "I do not know," said Richard. "I need to take her to the doctor." Within six months of that golf tournament, Beverly was diagnosed with Stage Three Alzheimer's. She was barely 62 years old.

Richard took care of her at home for the first year, utilizing adult day care services, but it was soon more than he could handle. Beverly was deteriorating rapidly and was incapable of doing anything for herself. Richard admitted her to a long-term care facility specializing in Alzheimer's patients, where she remained for the next eight years until her death.

Their insurance company paid out approximately $320,000 of claims over that period, a staggering amount of money for any family to absorb. Had they not been prepared with Long-Term Care coverage, Richard and Beverly would have run out of money in just over three years, being forced to spend down all their assets to qualify for Medicaid.

Remember, Beverly's ordeal lasted nearly ten years until her death, so their relatively sizeable assets would not have been enough. Without Long-Term Care Insurance, Richard would likely have had to sell their home and liquidate other assets, thereby compromising his quality of life, as well as bankrupting the legacy he and Beverly wanted to leave for their children.

The policy provided Richard with financial security, but more importantly, it gave him peace of mind knowing his wife was in a comfortable and reputable facility where she was treated with kindness, compassion, and dignity. Richard visited her nearly every day over those eight years, and he was able to maintain his own health and lifestyle, remaining in their home and taking comfort in knowing that his future was also secured.

Despite compelling stories like this, people still hesitate to 'gamble' on obtaining Long-Term Care Insurance. I tell my clients that there are four important reasons to plan for Long-Term Care Insurance: asset protection, asset preservation for future generations, financial independence, and maintaining your dignity. No parent wants to have to depend on their children to support them financially or have them be responsible for their daily care.

There are four major misconceptions people have about Long-Term Care Insurance, and they are my biggest challenges when advising clients. The first is that people think the premiums are too expensive. To that I say, "Would you still feel it is too expensive if I tell you we can use one percent of your net worth to provide all the coverage you will need to protect and preserve your assets?"

The second misconception is, "It will not happen to me." I wish that were the case, but statistics show that there is a 50/50 chance that after age 65, you and/or your spouse will require long-term care for a period of at least ninety days. Compare that to these statistics: the odds of your home burning down to the ground and being a complete loss is 1 in 1,000, yet everybody has Homeowners' Insurance and the average home value in the United States is approximately $120,000. The odds of you totaling your car are about 1 in 500, yet everybody has Auto Insurance and the average car is valued at approximately $12,000.

The third one is, "My kids or my spouse will take care of me." My first response is always, "What do your kids do? Where do they live?" More often than not, the children live a distance away, have full-time jobs, homes, and children of their own to care of. Even if the kids live locally, I ask, "Would you really want your son or daughter coming over to help you get dressed, bathed, fed, or help you use the bathroom? Do you not want to keep your independence and dignity?"

The fourth misconception is that the government (i.e. Medicare or Medicaid) will take care of me. Medicare only covers skilled nursing care for 100 days, and you have to "spend down" your assets to approximately $5,000 or less to qualify for Medicaid.

When people are confronted with the reality of that scenario, they begin to see the light. I do not recite these statistics and examples to scare people or push them into buying coverage they do not need; it's quite the opposite, in fact. My motto has always been, "I will not recommend Long-Term Care coverage unless they have adequate assets that need to be protected."

Long-Term Care Insurance is not a simple product, and that is why I stay abreast of the latest legislation and benefits available for me to educate my clients. I consider the company rating and something new called *partnership programs,* which gives the client a dollar-for-dollar credit based on what their policy has paid. Those assets are then protected from Medicaid should they ever have to spend down.

Other features include survivorship benefits, daily benefit minimums, and compound inflation riders, all designed to provide maximum coverage and peace of mind. And finally, there is the consideration of tax deductibility. Many clients are pleasantly surprised at how much of their Long Term Care premiums are tax deductible.

Just 15 or 20 years ago, it was legal to transfer assets to qualify for Medicaid coverage, as happened with a client of mine. He was a farmer and owned land, equipment, and a farmhouse at considerable value. When he retired, everything was kept in his name, though his son was running the farm. As fate would have it, about a year later, the retired farmer had a massive stroke, rendering him severely incapacitated and requiring extensive nursing home care.

While the man was in the hospital, his wife and son went to their attorney and legally transferred all of the assets to the son. When the nursing home inquired how he would be paying for his care, his wife answered, "We have no assets." They could document that everything was in his son's name, and therefore the farmer immediately qualified for Medicaid and their assets were protected.

This scenario would never happen today. As Medicaid has grown lower on funds, the laws surrounding transfer of assets have tightened. It was first changed to a two-year "look back" rule, meaning that for my farmer client, everything would have been needed to be transferred to his son a full two years before his illness. Only then would the assets be safe from reattachment by the nursing home. Now it has progressed to a five-year "look back" rule, and it is likely to increase.

It may sound insensitive, but the point of that legislation was to preserve Medicaid for those who truly have no money and cannot care for themselves; it is not meant for people of means to hide their assets. It is a different landscape from 20 years ago. Long-Term Care Insurance is now the most viable, legal avenue for people to protect and preserve their assets.

Nugget of Wisdom

In the simplest terms, you do not want to work your entire life, saving for your future, only to watch it disappear in five years. Does it not make sense to take less than one percent of your net worth to guarantee that the other 99 percent will not go to a long-term care facility?

About the Author

Dana F. Troske is the founder of Troske Financial Group, a comprehensive financial planning agency. With over 24 years of experience in the industry, Dana is committed to providing his clients with the most up-to-date products and services available, by staying ahead of the ever-changing landscape of insurance laws and regulations. This makes Dana uniquely qualified to evaluate your financial situation and determine the best way to insure your family's comfort, well-being, and peace of mind.

To reach Dana for a financial profile to assess your long-term care needs, contact him at (402) 465-5888, extension 222, or e-mail him at dana.tfg@adviserfocus.com

Dana F. Troske

Troske Financial Group

dana.tfg@adviserfocus.com

(402) 465-5888, extension 222

1(888) 305-8268 extension 222

"THAT REMINDS ME, I NEED TO SEE MY AGENT TOMORROW TO PURCHASE LIFE INSURANCE AND PROTECT MY FAMILY."

Image Courtesy cf CopyBoosters.com

No Substitute for the Personal Touch

By Kevin P. Pearce, LUTCF, FSS

Twenty years ago, a mutual acquaintance referred Ruth to me. The acquaintance knew Ruth wanted someone to help her handle her investments and plan for her future. Ruth's husband suffered from Parkinson's disease and was therefore no longer able to fully participate in the family's financial decisions, which meant Ruth had to take the reigns.

Ruth and her husband had saved a lot of wealth, although she they did not make much money. Old-fashioned through-and-through, they had saved and invested over the years and were sitting on a nice lump sum that was continuing to grow, albeit slowly.

To be honest, Ruth did not entirely trust me at first. She was fearful about sharing her financial information with a stranger, which is understandable. Eventually, she gave me access to a portion of her portfolio, just to see what I could do. Once she was confident in my abilities, we began discussing all her assets.

Those first few meetings involved discussions about annuities, mutual funds, you name it. We arranged for short-term care for her husband, whose health was failing.

I encouraged Ruth to purchase long-term care insurance in case she ever needed it. Being frugal and practical, she did not want to spend the money on premiums. Ruth was an office worker with a steady job. She had always been in good health. Why should she put money toward "nursing home insurance"? I outlined how easy it would be for Ruth to lose her life savings if she chose to do nothing; after realizing it would pay off, she finally agreed.

Over time, we created a total estate plan so Ruth could pass her wealth along to her daughter in the most tax-efficient way possible.

Tax efficiency is an attractive attribute. In Ruth's case, I involved her in tax-favored investments such as tax-deferred annuities and some tax-free bonds. This method of money management kept Ruth in a lower tax bracket; in fact, some of my clients are not even in tax brackets thanks to tax efficiency.

After many months, Ruth's husband's Parkinson's worsened to a critical point. He became unable to take care of himself, so I helped Ruth tap into their insurance to buy a hospital-type bed. Ruth cared for him at their home practically 24/7. She did not want to spend money unnecessarily on hospitalization, nor did she want strangers to watch over the man she loved.

When her husband passed away, he did so with his doting wife by his side. It was the way he wanted to spend his final days, and his contentment made Ruth's transition into widowhood a little easier. She was able to mourn without worrying about her financial future; after all, we had already taken care of the "what ifs."

A few years after her husband passed away, Ruth experienced health struggles of her own. One morning, she did not show up for work, which was highly unusual. Her colleagues became concerned and called the house, but no one answered. So they informed the police, who broke into Ruth's home. They found her unconscious on the floor, the victim of a brain aneurysm. The rescue squad was summoned and she was thankfully revived, but she needed to be placed in a nursing home.

Luckily, Ruth had all her bases covered. Long before her medical emergency, we had written an estate plan with the help of an attorney and an accountant. And remember that long-term care insurance? It is still paying for her nursing home care.

Ruth is not using any assets at all. Her daughter does not have to dip into her savings, either, which is a relief. That is something Ruth was clear about — that she would never be a burden on her daughter. By establishing an estate plan, I have made certain that Ruth can pass all her assets to her daughter and grandchildren.

Had Ruth waited and not sought out a relationship with a financial advisor until much later in her life, she would not have been eligible for nearly as many benefits. Certainly, she did not like spending money on long-term health insurance when she was fit and healthy, but she knew it was practical. In the end, she made the right choice.

Recently, Ruth moved to a different nursing home because the one she was living in was not meeting her expectations, nor was she getting the quality care she deserved. So her daughter and I worked together to move her to a better place.

Ruth is one tough lady. She has beaten death at least three times and worked through the difficult loss of her husband, yet is always upbeat and determined. I feel privileged to have been her advisor and friend for more than two decades.

As Ruth's case shows, long-term care insurance is one of the products that gives people the highest returns on their investment, not to mention peace of mind. I work with a third party that oversees the long-term care insurance that I recommend, and that company consistently provides exactly what my clients need.

But before any work is accomplished, a reciprocal trust must be developed between advisor and client. Those first few meetings with a financial advisor are much like interviews — for everyone. I look for quality clients, and clients look for quality financial advice. We begin to establish a relationship from day one. I try to be an open book, and I hope for the same from them. After we agree to work together, we can build a customized, flexible financial plan.

My process is simple and straightforward. I gather all the information I can for and from my clients. I examine the overall snapshot of a client's portfolio so I can best guide him or her. If someone comes to me with $50,000 worth of investments, I am going to suggest something totally different than I would for the person with $3 million in assets.

It is really no different than working with a CPA or family doctor — trust is vital. For instance, if a family doctor says you need to do something, you will most likely listen. It is the same thing in my industry. When I tell my clients that something is in their best interest, they have to trust me to believe that what I'm saying is true.

I get to know a client's life history. I try to understand where the client was raised, how they were raised, and what they want for their future. It is fascinating to glean information regarding my clients' backgrounds. Were their parents religious? Did their family believe in insurance? Did their mothers and fathers teach them anything about money? How about insurance?

I routinely ask clientele who and what in their lives have affected their financial decisions the most. What were the best financial decisions they ever made? What were the worst? What did they learn from their experiences? An open-format dialogue allows for unique discussions and better representation on my part.

This personalized approach gives me a basis for how we can most effectively work with one another. For example, if someone grew up wearing hand-me-down clothing and is comfortable with that lifestyle, I will usually make conservative or low-risk financial suggestions. On the other hand, if someone grew up in that same type of household but does not want to live like that as an adult, I may suggest more aggressive investment options. Knowing my clients' histories gives me a starting point of how much risk tolerance they have.

It is very, very important to find somebody you get along with because you will be assured that the advisor has your interests at heart. I have told prospective clientele many times that if they do not feel comfortable with me, they should seek out someone with whom they do.

Let's face it. You have to like the person you work with. You have to be able to look each other straight in the eye. I look at my clients square in the face and tell them what I recommend.

I am lucky enough to consider my clients as friends. We go out for dinner or meet for breakfast. In fact, I recently had a client stop by out of the blue with a bag of Starbucks coffee! It is times like those that I am so glad I chose this profession.

Nugget of Wisdom

I have to admit, financial advisors are a dime-a-dozen. Any Tom, Dick, or Harriet can call himself or herself a financial advisor. There are only so many mutual funds, so many stocks, so many life insurance policies on the market. What makes the difference is working with someone you trust.

About the Author

Kevin P. Pearce, LUTCF, FSS has been a financial advisor for over 23 years and currently owns Pearce Financial Services. He earned Life Underwriter Training Council Fellow and Financial Services Specialist degrees from the American College. Contact Kevin for a free consultation at: kevin.pfs@adviserfocus.com or (402) 502-6900.

Kevin P. Pearce

Pearce Financial Services

kevin.pfs@adviserfocus.com

(402) 502-6900

www.pearcefinancial.org

Everyone Can Live the American Dream

By Chris Casey

We can learn a lot from Ed and Jean, a "middle American" couple with two kids. Ed and Jean each worked for their respective employers (Ed for a university and Jean for a local school) for nearly three decades. Though they never made tons of money, they were diligent savers; if you met them, you would never guess how modest their combined income was for most of their marriage. Today, their combined income is finally over $100,000, but it wasn't that high when they first started their family.

Yet despite their modest finances, Ed, 62, and Jean, 61, sent their children through private school and even paid for half of each of their children's college tuition. They bought their own house and nearly have the mortgage paid off. In fact, Ed told me that when he purchased his home, he did so with a down payment of 25 percent. With admiration, I told him that was unheard of today.

Ed and Jean always gave back to their church as well as their community. They saved conscientiously, even if they could only put aside $25 or $50 a month. Even so, they took yearly vacations, which, though not luxurious, were just what the family needed. They engaged in what I consider a healthy concept of "save some, share some, spend some" and it trickled down to both their children.

What Ed and Jean did isn't magic, though it might seem unbelievable to people. It is just practicing the fundamentals of money management. You don't over leverage yourself. You don't drive a car you can't afford. You don't spend money you don't have.

As Ed once said to me, "If your income is less than your expenses, you have a problem. If your income is more than your expenses, you're doing all right." It's all very common sense, but I have to say I don't see it happening as much as I wish I did. There's plenty of credit card and other types of debt out there; in fact, it's become the norm for many people to live outside of their means.

Most people would look at Ed and Jean's situation and assume they're set for life. They have a retirement nest egg now and are financially stable for the foreseeable future. So why should they contact a financial advisor like me?

The answer is simple, especially to folks like Ed and Jean who live for today but save for tomorrow. Even though they were sitting on a nice, comfortable retirement account, they were sensible enough to know that they needed a professional's help to prepare for those years when they'd no longer be working. That's why they turned to me to help secure their retirement years by constructing a personalized portfolio.

To satisfy Ed and Jean's desire to make their money "work" for them after they retire, I examined both the insurance and investment side of their current financial plan. I made certain any measures we took would be in sync with their Social Security and pension income streams that they'll receive.

As I mentioned before, my work was made easier thanks to their practicality. For a long time, they had contributed to their employer retirement programs, both 403(b)s. Each would contribute what he or she could and stretch enough so that, as Ed put it, they could "feel the pain ... just a little bit." By investing in 403(b)s, their dollars were coming out pre-tax, a nice advantage.

The three of us sat down several times after we initially met. We designed a thorough plan so we could project their standard of living desires 10, 20, maybe 30 years down the road. Naturally, they told me they wanted to maintain their same lifestyle. They'd spent 40 years building up their savings, and they weren't about to change their levelheaded financial habits.

I evaluated whether they would have enough assets to keep those standards of living by using their pension income, projected Social Security income, and retirement savings. I also looked at what types of income streams they would need in the coming decades by projecting inflation rates. We methodically ran through several scenarios with various rates of return and inflation increases. Then we set in motion investments that would pay off steadily and reliably.

At this point, we've programmed guaranteed income streams so Ed and Jean can keep their same standard of living. And the rest of their assets are going to grow predictably. That way, they're not going to have to worry about touching those assets

— but if they need to, they can. If an emergency occurs, they'll be protected.

I have to say that Ed and Jean are favorite clients of mine. As they've proven, every little bit adds up — their personal balance sheet is truly amazing. They've done so much of the groundwork in terms of being sensible that it's made my job a pure pleasure. But I must admit that they're also tough as nails — they want to know that every penny they invest with me is maximized and that their financial advisor is trustworthy. I've been honored to represent them.

Do Ed and Jean still have money concerns? Of course. They are worried about health care costs in the future. They have concerns that pension benefits have the possibility of being reduced. They are also apprehensive about a drastic change in Social Security. But we've set up a fairly conservative financial plan, so we've minimized much of the risk.

Even when the economy has dipped, Ed and Jean haven't batted an eye now that we've diversified their overall financial plan on both the insurance and the investment side. They know that with the planning we've done, the market's fluctuations will have very little impact on their lives.

I use Ed and Jean as examples when I speak with new and prospective clients, regardless of their ages. After all, Ed and Jean are proof that living simply doesn't have to involve tremendous sacrifice or hardship.

A lot of the clients I work with are from middle America, meaning their incomes are very average. To get things started, I suggest the first step they take is allocating something for the future, enough so that they feel the "pain" just a little bit. I also suggest they allocate some money for the present, like vacations. If people are so inclined, we talk about allocating something to organizations that could use their financial support. This is the simple concept of "save some, spend some, share some."

When an individual appears panicked at the thought of changing his or her spending habits, I suggest we start with something small, like saving a reasonable amount from each paycheck. I don't want to police his or her personal situation … but I do want to be a responsible consultant, which involves telling clientele the right thing to do.

I help people plan for retirement, even if it's 30 years away. My mission is to protect what's really important. Therefore, I assist clients in making sure all their belongings go to the people they designate, just in case the unexpected happens. I also help put clients' kids through college without breaking the proverbial bank.

It's an exciting business — I deal with a lot of the "what ifs" in life. I provide investment services and insurance products, but I also provide my own expertise in projecting how to keep more of their money safe and available over the long run. Save some, share some, spend some, it's the way I run my business, and my wife and I run our household, and I know it works.

As far as I'm concerned, a large part of my role is as a financial consultant, and I take that seriously. If I notice something amiss on a client's tax return, I'll arrange for a meeting with a professional I trust. If my clients are already working with someone they trust, I'll call that person to arrange a sit-down meeting just to be sure we have a coordinated plan. It's all about taking the worry out of planning for people and building long-term relationships.

When people pick a financial advisor, they should choose someone they trust, someone who will sit down with them often. If you can't remember the last time you sat down with your financial advisor, that's a red flag. Seek out help from somebody who truly cares and will educate you about our complex financial world. There are so many products, so many services … it can get confusing. Find someone you connect with.

There has to be a relationship on both sides of the equation. The advisor has to want the client and vice versa. Over the years, the relationship should develop into a partnership where the advisor knows what's truly important to the client. It is (and should be) a very intimate partnership.

Nugget of Wisdom

Save some, share some, spend some. Six simple words, but they're incredibly powerful.

In today's "spend some, spend some, spend some" world, it can all become too one dimensional. There must be balance. Saving, sharing, and spending are concepts that help provide this balance.

About the Author

Chris Casey has been serving the Twin Cities and surrounding areas in Minnesota since 2006. He holds a bachelor's degree in accounting and is a certified public accountant. He entered the financial services profession with a strong desire to help clients identify and achieve those financial goals most important to them.

Chris offers a free, no-obligation financial consultation to individuals and families who want to define their dreams and goals and take their financial responsibilities seriously. Meetings can be held in person at his office in Bloomington, Minnesota or via telephone. Contact him at chris.casey@adviserfocus.com or (952) 888-2772, ext. 230.

Chris Casey

chris.casey@adviserfocus.com

(952) 888-2772, ext. 230

Protecting and Nurturing the Memories

By Andrew C. Rodriguez, LUTCF

Parents go to great lengths to provide the absolute best for their children. The goal is simple: to give their children more than they had growing up. George and Margie Sampson weren't any different than other parents in their desire to give their children as much as they could. Together, they created a loving environment where childhood memories were nurtured.

George was a hard-working, commercial roofer in the Boston area. Margie was a homemaker who loved to entertain. In addition to their five children, they acted as "parents" to many neighborhood children — five — keeping them occupied and out of trouble. I was one of those children and my parents became close friends with George and Margie Sampson. The neighborhood was like a big family. That's just the way it was growing up in Somerville, Massachusetts.

In 1958, George and Margie bought a vacation home in Wareham, Massachusetts, along Swifts Beach. They wanted a weekend and summer home where their family could retreat from the city. And being the close friends that we were, it wasn't too long after that my parents bought their vacation home a few doors down from the Sampsons.

As the area became a hot spot for vacationers, George seized the opportunity to invest in property. He bought a second cottage along the beach and a collection of fourteen small cottages, known as "The Village." The properties served as a source of income for the family, and with each addition of property, George increased his assets and wealth.

As a child, I remember everyone working together to tidy up the rental properties for the vacationers. Every Saturday after "check out," the families helped each other clean the cottages for the next renters who would arrive later that afternoon. Everyone helped, and every week we got it done without many complaints. It was part of living along the shores of Swifts Beach during the summer and just one of many memories we all share.

After I became an adult, George and Margie became my clients, and I advised them on some of their investments. One day they mentioned to me that they'd met with an insurance agent from another company. The insurance agent recommended they purchase a life insurance policy to protect their assets. Even George and Margie recognized that purchasing a single life insurance policy wasn't going to protect their entire estate. They had several properties and other assets that they'd worked hard to acquire and preserve over the years. A "one-policy-protects-all" solution simply wasn't the answer. That's when they turned to me for advice.

After this experience, George and Margie realized they needed to work with someone they trusted — someone who understood just how important it was to preserve their assets. The cottages along Swifts Beach weren't just property or just assets. They were wrapped in decades of memories. Together, we started mapping out a plan to preserve their estate and those memories.

George and Margie's goal was to keep the real estate along Swifts Beach in the family. They didn't want their children to ever face needing to sell even a portion to cover estate taxes or probate costs. There was summer after summer of family memories tied to those cottages in Wareham, and they wanted their children to have the opportunity to continue to make more memories with their families.

There were several steps to accomplishing this goal. First, I recommended George and Margie purchase a "second to die" life insurance policy, which covers a couple and pays on the second death, not the first. Because the insurance company pays only on the second death, the premiums on a "second to die" policy cost less than two individual life insurance policies, which makes it an attractive option in estate planning. "Second to die" policies are also useful for a couple where one may have more health issues than the other because the insurance carrier is reviewing the life expectancy of both persons.

Second, I arranged for George and Margie to meet with an attorney, who specializes in estate planning, to conduct an assets analysis. It is extremely important to work with a attorney throughout the planning process because it helps clients take advantage of the Tax Code. More of their assets get passed to their heirs, not the IRS. Once the analysis was complete, the assets were split equally between George and Margie (to take advantage of the tax code), and three trusts were established —

one for George, one for Margie, and one for the second-to-die life insurance. Moreover, these trusts were all designed so that once both parents passed on, they would distribute to the children.

Because the trust for George and the trust for Margie each was "revocable", changes could be made to these trusts while they were still alive. In fact, even though the trust of the first-to-die became "irrevocable" upon death, the survivor actually was able to use a power-of-appointment to re-direct how that trust ultimately distributed to the children and grandchildren. Generally speaking, however, upon death, these trusts become "irrevocable" so that the wishes of the deceased would be carried out.

Had George and Margie not planned their estate in this fashion, their children could have lost many of the assets they'd grown to love over the years. However, the "second to die" life insurance policy and tax advantages of the trusts prevented any losses of childhood memories. The death benefit paid Margie's medical expenses and some other outstanding debt upon her death. The rest of the money was used to make modifications to a few cottages in "The Village" so that George and Margie's children could build a new generation of family memories.

During the planning process, the biggest concern any client has is ensuring that assets are not tied up in probate. They don't want their children burdened with the emotional stress and additional costs associated with probate. Any assets that are not contained within a trust go through probate — even those mentioned in a will. The time it takes to validate a will through probate can take months or even a year or more — delaying the passing of your hard-earned assets from being passed to your children. Unfortunately, this can actually result in lost assets. Between probate fees and attorney fees, transferring your assets might cost your children anywhere from three to six percent of the total assets. By setting up a trust, you can avoid the probate process for many of your assets, and it gives your heirs access to your estate.

For George and Margie, this is where the "second to die" life insurance policy came into play. After Margie's death, the policy paid out to their children, which gave them money to cover the last expenses and estate taxes. This freed up George and Margie's assets so their children could begin enjoying them. Without the money necessary to cover the last expenses and any estate taxes, the assets would have been untouchable until those expenses were covered. That's not the burden any parent wants to leave to their children.

Nugget of Wisdom

Planning is a must-do if you want to have a say in what happens to your estate. Not only are you protecting yourself while you are alive, but you also are protecting your children.

About the Author

Andrew C. Rodriguez has been in the business of helping people protect their lives and plan for their retirement since 1981. Andy helps his clients discover the right array of tools to serve their needs, including life insurance and long-term care insurance. Through the years he's assisted many families with retirement planning and estate preservation.

If you are interested in learning more about Andy's products and services, contact him at (508) 295-0405 or andrew.rodriguez@adviserfocus.com

Andrew C. Rodriguez, LUTCF

andrew.rodriguez@adviserfocus.com

(508) 295-0405

"CONGRATULATIONS ED, THIS LIFE INSURANCE POLICY GUARANTEES YOUR CHILDREN'S EDUCATION."

Image Courtesy of CopyBoosters.com

Armor of Protection

By Michael G. Collins
Collins Financial Group, Inc.

It isn't every day that you meet someone with whom you can instantly strike up a friendship, but that's how it was when I met my neighbor, Chuck. We got to know him and his family and soon realized we had a lot in common. He was a big hockey fan, so we'd go to hockey games together, and our families socialized as well. Being a firefighter, Chuck also had a "second family," his firefighter family, and I soon became friends with his fellow firefighters and was often included in their outings.

One night, Chuck and I were watching a football game and the subject of life insurance came up. He mentioned that he had some coverage through work, but he admitted it probably wasn't enough. Consequently, we decided to make an appointment to take a look at his coverage and talk some more … during business hours, not during the game.

Chuck and his wife, Marie, weren't unlike many couples. They were unsure about the scores of insurance products available, and when they did purchase life insurance, they never continued with the premium payments — for a variety of reasons. Perhaps it was because they were unsure of the product they'd purchased, or they simply didn't feel comfortable with the salesperson. When we reviewed his insurance coverage, my question to Chuck was simple: What was the most important thing he wanted covered should something happen to him?

As a firefighter, Chuck was not blind to death. He worked on the hazardous materials (HAZMAT) team and was also an emergency medical technician (EMT). He knew that he was putting himself at risk every time he was called to duty. Additionally, he knew that in his line of work, the chance of something tragic happening was greater for him than for the average man sitting at a desk all day.

Even so, there were also great benefits in being a firefighter. Because of the unique shift schedule of a firefighter, Chuck would work a few days straight and then have a few days off.

This allowed him the time to enjoy his other passion: his family. He helped his kids with their homework, and both kids were competitive swimmers, so he spent much of his time off attending their swim practices and meets at the local YMCA. He was often called "Mr. Mom" and wore that title with great pride and honor.

Because we were friends, I already knew the answer to my question. I wasn't surprised at all when Chuck replied, "My family is the most important thing to me." He wanted to be sure that should something happen to him, his wife and kids would be taken care of — that they wouldn't have to move and that the kids could attend college. He had one life insurance policy through work, but after sitting with me, he realized that policy wasn't enough to accomplish what was most important for him — caring for his family should something happen to him. That's why he was having this conversation with me, and together, we selected the right policy to fit his needs.

In May 2003, Chuck visited the doctor to have a cyst removed near his eye. The tests concluded the cyst was malignant; he had cancer. Subsequent testing showed that the cancer was in his lung, on his liver, and he had developed tumors on his brain.

His doctors recommended surgery immediately, but Chuck elected to postpone. It was the end of the school year, Father's Day was just a few weeks after that, and he didn't want to ruin those times for his kids. He elected to wait until after Father's Day to tell his children and have the surgery. At this time, the prognosis was grim; he was given a year to live.

In total, Chuck had eleven tumors removed from his brain, which left one side of his body paralyzed. But Chuck was a warrior. While still in the hospital after his last surgery, he would try to lift his arm up over his head just to show that he was gaining progress. He never gave up the fight.

During one of my visits with him in the hospital, Chuck asked, "Mike, am I truly covered? Is my family really going to get the money?" I assured him that yes, indeed, he was covered.

Then he told me about one time when he wanted to play golf. Money was a little tight that month, and his firefighter buddies had invited him to play. He really wanted to go. "I almost cancelled the policy so I'd have the money to play golf," he confided. "How would I feel now if I had cancelled the policy so I could golf?"

Chuck passed away in June of 2004 — almost exactly a year after he was diagnosed with cancer. After Chuck's death, his fifteen-year-old son pulled me aside to tell me that he was so thankful that he didn't have to move, that they could stay in their home. The family could have a bit of normalcy to get them through this loss … all because Chuck had planned appropriately.

For most people, life insurance is an intangible thing. You can't touch it and show it off to your friends like you could if you'd purchased a fancy new car or a huge plasma TV. Life insurance is an unselfish purchase. It is something that nobody knows you have other than yourself and your family. But it is a very rewarding purchase. It rewards you by knowing that, should something happen to you, your loved ones are taken care of. In fact, one of the biggest benefits of life insurance is simply peace of mind.

Often, procrastination gets the best of us and causes us not to want to think about "that bad stuff." This is especially true for couples who are young and healthy. After seeing what happened to my client and friend, Chuck, I now feel it is my duty to be more aggressive in educating people on the importance of planning. When life is going along good and you are engrossed in your career, family, and extracurricular activities, people don't want to stop and plan for a catastrophe. I get that. But the reality is that tragedy can happen at any time. Wouldn't you want to have that peace of mind by knowing you are taking care of your loved ones?

My advice to someone who wants to discuss insurance is this: find someone who will look at your entire picture and not someone who is simply trying to sell you a "one-size-fits-all" product. Some questions you need to be able to answer for yourself include: what are your goals, what do you want to accomplish by acquiring this type of insurance, and what are you truly trying to achieve?

Further, it isn't simply about needing life insurance, although that is one element in the overall equation of financial security. To be smart about the future, you need to plan for all of the possibilities, not simply one scenario. Besides the scenario of "What happens if I die?" there are other equally important scenarios: What happens if I live to be 100? What happens if I am disabled? At what age do I want to retire and how do I want to live my retirement years? The answers to these questions lead us down different paths that a client could potentially face at one point of his or her life. And to be smart about it, you need to plan for each potential situation, because we simply don't know which scenarios you'll face during your lifetime.

For me to successfully help a client achieve all of their goals, I spend a lot of time asking questions and listening to them. This helps me find the holes in their armor to make sure that we can protect what is most important to them.

Nugget of Wisdom

Enjoy today, but prepare for tomorrow.

About the Author

Michael G. Collins has been in the retirement planning and insurance business since 1980. He is the Founder and President of Collins Financial Group, Inc. and is a Life Member of the Million Dollar Roundtable. Because Mike knows that every client is different, he doesn't try to make a round peg fit into a square hole. He is diligent in locating the right product to fit his client's needs and in plugging up any hole in his client's "armor" to help make sure they have financial security.

Contact Mike to receive your complimentary, no-obligation checkup at (414) 359-1790 or mike.cfg@adviserfocus.com, and discover how to reinforce your armor of protection.

Michael G. Collins

Collins Financial Group, Inc.

11270 W. Park Place Suite 980

Milwaukee, WI 53224

mike.cfg@adviserfocus.com

(414) 359-1790

Following the Financial Path to Success

By Ron Fossum, CMP, RFC

When I first met Beau, he was a single guy making about $13 per hour as an employee and in debt about $40,000. Having recently been through a difficult divorce, he was essentially starting his life over. He came to my house to fix my car windshield, and we began to talk.

That was seven years ago. Today, Beau is the owner of a million-dollar business and multiple properties; he has been married to Joy for six years and is approaching a million dollars of net worth. How did he make such a dramatic transition so quickly?

Not everyone is willing to put in the effort it takes to create that kind of wealth so quickly, but my team can provide everything a person needs to reach his or her goals, however extravagant or modest they may be. Even though my team and I are helping people gain and maintain financial wealth, we understand the importance of separating *net*-worth from *self*-worth. We encourage our clients to focus on what they truly want — then we figure out how to create that long-term high quality of life through financial security.

As for Beau, there were some tough spots along the way, but he and I worked through those times and followed the plan we'd created together.

Beau wasn't my typical client when we first met. He was in his early twenties, had a negative net worth, and was considering starting his own business. More importantly, it was obvious he was very motivated to live a balanced life, following the values he'd been raised with.

To go out on his own with his automotive glass business, Beau first needed health insurance, which I helped him with. From there, it took a little convincing for him to understand that I was much more than a health insurance guy, but once I showed him how making a health insurance decision could positively or negatively influence all other areas of his financial plan, he quickly and eagerly surrendered to the financial planning process.

We started with a "goals and needs analysis," then bridged into investments and started filling in the holes. Our relationship grew as his company grew, and my company has advised him on everything from a business plan, personal and business cash flow, to life insurance, critical illness insurance, and disability insurance, and college planning for his child. We have also helped him sell his first home, buy his dream home and vacation home, and purchase five rental properties – in a way that enhanced his goals even more quickly.

Beau is enjoying his success now, with a beautiful home and several cars, as well as the means to travel. But he's also planning for his future. His goal is to retire before he reaches age 50, which he should be able to accomplish easily.

One transitional time for Beau was when he expanded his business from one employee to two. It was difficult because he needed to find just the right person for a relatively new company. By establishing a business plan and employee policies, we helped him figure it out, and today he has six employees, is planning to add two more, and is working toward becoming a "business owner" instead of being "self-employed." The difference, you ask? A business owner can depend on the business operating successfully without him being there every day, whereas a self-employed person has simply created a job for themselves.

My clients know that I am always looking out for their best interests, so they often check with me before making any big business or personal financial decisions. It's important to recognize that sometimes the route to a goal may change, and that's okay, as long as the client is aware of the consequences of that change. I'd rather plan than react, but life doesn't always work that way.

For example, Beau and Joy once called me when they were vacationing in Hawaii; they were in the company of a real estate agent. In their well-tuned personal financial agenda was the plan to purchase a second "vacation" home in three to five years, but they had found their dream home and were ready to purchase it immediately! They understood that making that big of a financial decision at a different time than we had discussed was going to affect everything else. They weren't looking for approval from me; they just wanted to know what the consequences could be. Specifically, the question from Beau was: "How much longer will I have to work?"

Within three days, I had rewritten their long-term plan to show how the purchase of this second home earlier than anticipated would affect their overall financial picture. From this information, Beau and Joy could make a sound decision. Beau understood that the change delayed his retirement date by about 3.2 years, but he was fine with that. They now had the vacation property of their dreams!

Beau and Joy and I have built up a level of trust between us. Beau knows I'm committed to his long-term success, not just making a quick profit, and Joy has told me she gets a real sense of serenity knowing they can come to me with any business or personal financial decisions, and get an honest and professional answer that fits in with their ultimate goals and values.

Joy once said she felt as if she and Beau were making fragmented financial decisions before they became my clients. They would go to their investment advisor for a piece of advice, their attorney for another, and their insurance agent for still another. No one was looking at the whole picture; each was looking at his own piece of the pie.

I introduced Beau to a process that my company developed, called Strategic Wealth Solutions. Working through the process helps clients coordinate and make smarter choices with all of their money decisions. We like to say that money doesn't come with instructions. Thus, we help our clients gain clarity and focus by making smarter choices with their money.

Beau and Joy's situation isn't unique. Because I have a personal interest in my clients achieving their financial goals, I've spent countless hours advising them on issues that I don't directly handle or receive compensation for. But it all dramatically enhances their chances of success, and that's what creates the "one-stop shopping" for all their financial needs. It is important to understand that any one recommendation can influence whether or not a client attains his or her goals, and ultimately success.

Smart Money Financial Group specializes in working with business owners, widows, retirees, and pre-retirees completely committed to a life of financial independence. We look for clients who are open minded to new ideas, and are action oriented and ready to implement the plans we help them create. In fact, that's one of the biggest benefits of using a financial firm that takes a team approach: the client gets a unique skill set and base of experience, from several team members, helping them through the total financial process and moving them closer to financial independence.

It's also equally important to choose a financial professional who is not partial to any one product, company, industry, or type of investing. If a planner only represents one company or product, it is only natural that they would try to push clients toward that company or product — which isn't always in the clients' best interests. My company focuses on both assets and liabilities, because both can positively or negatively impact your goals or success. Our approach is to go one step at a time, customizing a plan for each client based on his or her short- and long-term goals, and what is most important to them.

In the end, I always emphasize a team approach for anyone considering a financial advisor, because financial planning encompasses so many areas in both business and personal planning. No one can be an expert in every field. It is vital to look at the complete picture, not simply a piece or two, to both build up client's assets and also reduce or eliminate their liabilities.

Nugget of Wisdom

If you are casual about your finances … you will become a financial casualty! Take action today!

About the Author

Ron Fossum is a managing partner of Smart Money Financial Group, whose mission is to create an environment that allows the client to translate their goals to a custom-written financial strategy in order to fund a life of complete financial independence, as defined by the client. Ron created his unique five-step process, Strategic Wealth Solutions, designed to align a client's highest values and goals into a written strategy.

To learn about his cutting-edge strategies or receive the free CD, "Your Financial Future – Choice or Chance?" contact Ron at (888) 560-7119 or visit www.smartmoneyfinancialgroup.com.

Ron Fossum, CMP, RFC
Smart Money Financial Group
www.smartmoneyfinancialgroup.com
(888) 560-7119

YOUR FINANCIAL PLANNER
IS A BRIDGE TO HELPING
SECURE YOUR FAMILY'S FUTURE.

Image Courtesy of CopyBoosters.com

APPENDIX 1

Are There Any White Hats Left?

Don Connelly

I recently read an article comparing today's FBI involvement in The Meltdown versus the FBI's involvement in the S & L scandal of the late 1980's and the early 1990's. According to a recent USA Today article, the total loss in the S & L scandal was more than $150 billion versus more than $1 trillion today. Yet the number of agents assigned to the task then was more than 1,000 versus only 240 agents working on today's crisis. The difference of course has everything to do with today's increased emphasis on national security. Additional agents will be assigned to the financial crisis, because according to the FBI, there are currently 530 corporate-fraud cases pending, 38 of which relate directly to the meltdown.

Bad news sells. Reporters everywhere must be standing on their desks and thanking the journalism gods for such job security. The Germans call it Schadenfreude.

Unfortunately for the rest of us, mainstream media people make their living bottom fishing. They don't make any money printing good news. So don't expect a break.

There was a destination on the White House website that I presume is gone today. That section told you one hundred things you didn't know about the George Bush administration. To say good things about George Bush would not have furthered the agendas of mainstream media and would not have sold any newspapers. Hence those one hundred things never saw the light of day. For the same reasons, good things about our industry are never going to see the light of day. So I'm going to tell you a few good things about good people that would never sell newspapers.

Bernie sells newspapers. Bernie Madoff wiped out charities, he ruined lives and, if he hadn't been caught, he'd still be doing it. He's a sociopath. He destroys lives. And he sells a lot of newspapers.

Ed does not. Ed is a Financial Advisor in Western Pennsylvania. Ed's widowed client asked Ed to go with her when she bought a new car. She knew which car she wanted. She didn't need Ed's help with that. It seems that her late husband had taught her to be wary of people selling cars, so she felt that Ed's just being there would afford her some measure of peace of mind. Ed told me that he goes to clients' real estate closings. His capacity is unofficial. It's just that his presence gives his clients comfort. Every year Ed treats his clients to an evening of dinner, dancing and socializing at the local Ramada Inn. Ed's wife's family owns that Ramada Inn. The clients show up in droves because they like being around Ed and his wife. I saw that with my own eyes at Ed's 25th year-in-the-business celebration. He is a kind and gentle soul. He enriches lives. But his deeds are not considered newsworthy. Ed doesn't sell any newspapers at all. Therefore your clients will never hear of Ed. But they'll sure know a lot about Bernie.

Art gets ratings. Art Nadel is in jail in Florida, accused of stealing $350 million in a Ponzi scheme. He was tracked down and caught in flight, after faking his own suicide. He wiped out charities, he ruined lives and, if he hadn't been caught, he'd still be doing it. He's a sociopath. He destroys lives. And he sells a lot of newspapers.

Duane does not. Duane is a Financial Advisor in the Pacific Northwest. Every fall Duane calls his older clients to remind them that they are not to venture out when conditions are icy. Duane and his wife run errands for these clients because they feel it's the right thing to do. Every year Duane has a dinner to honor those clients who gave him referrals during the year. He is a kind and gentle soul. He enriches lives. But his deeds are not considered newsworthy. Duane doesn't sell any newspapers at all. Therefore your clients will never hear of Duane. But they'll sure know a lot about Art.

The press loves Marcus. Marcus Schrenker sits in the Pensacola Escambia County jail accused of faking his own death, as authorities closed in on him for his part in an annuity churning scam. To avoid arrest, Schrenker made a phony distress call from his airplane, parachuted to safety and let the plane crash 100 yards from occupied houses. He then fled on a motorcycle he had stashed away. He was dumb enough to leave in the cockpit an atlas and a campground directory with the Florida and Alabama pages missing from both. As authorities closed in on him, he slit a wrist. He is as bad as it gets. He ruined lives and, if he hadn't been caught, he'd still be doing it. He's a sociopath. He destroys lives. And he sells a lot of newspapers.

They don't care about Tom. Tom has hired a social worker at his own expense. The social worker goes around in the morning to make sure Tom's older clients get their meds right. Tom feels that, in many cases, the Financial Advisor has replaced the minister in the home. His clients confide in him with utmost trust. He is treated as a trusted family friend. He is a kind and gentle soul. He enriches lives. But his deeds are not considered newsworthy. Tom doesn't sell any newspapers at all. Therefore your clients will never hear of Tom. But they'll sure know a lot about Marcus.

The cameras love Sir Allen. Sir Allen Stanford would normally just be considered a vain, insecure egomaniac if he hadn't ripped of billions of dollars and tried to flee the country after being charged with massive, ongoing fraud. There is also suspicion of money laundering. His demise began when his credit card was refused by a charter company as he apparently was trying to flee the country on a private jet. The need to feed his ego led to a $9.2 Billion fraud. He ruined lives and, if he hadn't been caught, he'd still be doing it. He's a sociopath. He destroys lives. And he sells a lot of newspapers.

They don't love Richard. Richard is a Financial Advisor and a humanitarian. He saw in his own family a tragic medical mishap lead to a large cash settlement. The cash settlement didn't last very long. Richard saw firsthand that people who obtain a lot of money quickly often don't deal well with their new found riches. Richard also knows that tragedy and grief are too large a price to pay. Money cannot compensate for ruined lives. Drawing upon personal experience, Richard incorporated grief counseling into his Financial Services practice. He has since mended many families both emotionally and financially. He has enhanced many lives over the years. He is a kind and gentle soul. He enriches lives. But his deeds are not considered newsworthy. Richard doesn't sell any newspapers at all. Therefore your clients will never hear of Richard. But they'll sure know a lot about Sir Allen.

Reporters want interviews with Ken, Dennis, and Mark. Ken Lay redefined corporate scandal and accounting fraud as he toppled Enron. Dennis Kozlowski and Mark Swartz made Tyco famous just before being sent up the river for twenty five years. They ruined lives and, if they hadn't been caught, they'd have kept it up. They are sociopaths. They destroyed lives. And they sold a lot of newspapers.

They don't want to talk to Carolyn. Carolyn is a Financial Advisor in the greater Houston area. Carolyn does pro bono financial planning for people who cannot afford a Financial Planner. In more than a few cases, Carolyn's financial help consists of fighting for benefits that these people deserve but would never get otherwise. She balances check books. She helps people get debit cards. She sets up college savings plans. She arranges for car loans. And she asks for nothing in return. She is Santa Claus and she is the Good Samaritan. She is a kind and gentle soul. She enriches lives. But her deeds are not considered newsworthy. Therefore your clients will never hear of Carolyn. But they'll sure know a lot about Ken and Dennis and Mark and Adelphia and Arthur Andersen and WorldCom and Global Crossing.

Or Bill. Bill is a life insurance agent in Australia. With ING's help, Bill delivered the proceeds from a life insurance policy to a 46-year old, terminally ill client; and then watched the client sob with appreciation and relief, secure in the knowledge that his two young daughters were now financially sound. I bet you have never heard of Bill.

There are a lot of white hats out there. I could go on and on with these examples. There are a lot more good guys in our industry than bad guys. There are lots of white hats out there. Our industry is full of good people and the press does not care.

But you and I care. And our families care. And our clients care. And all the people we help care.

Good guys may not be newsworthy, but they are kind and gentle souls who enrich lives. May you always be one of the good guys.

Throughout the past 40 years Don Connelly has been associated with Wall Street he has been a stockbroker, financial planner, branch manager, wholesaler, national sales manager, and for nearly 20 years, was a company spokesperson and Senior V.P. of Putnam Investments. In wide demand as a motivational speaker and trainer, Don has become known as a powerful beacon of wisdom to investors and financial services professionals in the United States and abroad.

PHIL'S WORKING WITH A FINANCIAL PLANNER HELPED HIM NAVIGATE HIS RETIREMENT.

Image Courtesy of CopyBoosters.com

APPENDIX 2

Claiming Life Insurance Benefits

Life insurance benefits are not paid automatically. If you are the beneficiary of a life insurance policy, you must file a claim in order to receive any money. Often, this is as simple as contacting your insurance agent and the deceased's employer and filling out some paperwork. You will need to provide each insurance company with a certified copy of the death certificate.

However, if this is the only step you take, you may be missing out on other life insurance benefits to which you are entitled if you fail to locate all of the life insurance benefits that the deceased was entitled to. If you spend time uncovering these hidden policies, you may end up with a great deal more money from life insurance than you expected.

Finding individually owned life insurance policies

Your spouse or family member may have owned one or more permanent or term life insurance policies. Individually owned term or permanent policies are what most people think of as life insurance. These policies are purchased by one person and pay benefits when the insured person dies. If your spouse or family member owned one of these policies, he or she probably kept it with his or her important papers in a file or in a safe-deposit box.

However, if you know that your spouse or family member owned an individual policy and you can't find it, call his or her insurance agent or company to check. It may be wise to review canceled checks to see if you can locate any premium payments to insurance companies. If you know that there was a policy but you can't find it, check the Internet or call your state insurance department for the names of companies that may, for a fee, help you locate a policy.

Finding group life insurance policies

Group life insurance policies provide coverage to many people under one policy. Group insurance policies may be issued through an employer, bank, credit agency, or other professional or social organizations, and they often pay benefits in specialized circumstances. Because the group holds the actual policy, the insured person receives a certificate of insurance as proof that he or she is insured. Look for these certificates in your spouse's or family member's personal papers, files, and safe-deposit box. If you can't find any certificates, this doesn't mean that your spouse wasn't insured. You should still check with your spouse's or family member's employer, bank, or credit agency, or study loan paperwork or purchase contracts. Read the following sections for information about types of group policies that your spouse or family member may have owned.

Employer-based group life insurance

If your spouse or family member was employed at the time of his or her death, you may be the beneficiary of a life insurance policy issued through his or her employer. Because some employers offer their employees a certain amount of life insurance at no cost, you may not even be aware that your spouse or family member was insured by a group policy because he or she did not pay his or her own premiums. What's more, your spouse or family member may have had the option of purchasing additional group life insurance through his or her employer, paying the extra premiums himself or herself. So, before assuming that your spouse or family member did not have group life insurance, you should check his or her pay stubs and call his or her employer.

Accidental death and dismemberment policy

Your spouse or family member may have been offered an accidental death and dismemberment policy through an employer, credit card, or bank. These policies pay benefits if an insured individual dies accidentally. This is another type of life insurance you may be unaware that your spouse or family member had because, occasionally, these policies are offered as part of a loan package or even issued as a free benefit by banks or as a rider to an employer-issued insurance policy. If your spouse or family member died accidentally, look for such a policy in his or her files, or contact his or her employer, bank, credit card issuer, or insurance company.

Travel accident insurance

If your spouse or family member was killed while traveling by air, boat, or train, you may be eligible to receive the proceeds from a travel accident insurance policy that he or she may have purchased when buying tickets. In addition, if your spouse or family member used a credit card to purchase travel tickets, you may be automatically entitled to a life insurance benefit payable if he or she dies as a result of an accident when using those tickets. Some travel agencies and road and travel clubs also routinely issue travel accident insurance policies, and employers sometimes pay death benefits to employees who are killed while traveling on company business.

Mortgage life insurance

If your spouse or family member owned a house, he or she may have purchased mortgage life insurance. A mortgage life insurance policy pays off the balance of the policyholder's mortgage upon his or her death. If you're not sure whether your spouse or family member purchased such a policy, check with the mortgage lender.

Credit life insurance

Banks and finance companies routinely offer credit life insurance when someone takes out a loan or is issued a line of credit. This insurance will pay off the outstanding balance of a loan or account if the insured individual dies. A few extra dollars are added to the monthly loan payments to pay the premiums. Because this type of policy is so profitable for the bank or finance company, most institutions try to sell it when someone finances a purchase or signs up for a line of credit, and occasionally they add it to a contract before the individual signs the contract. So, it's likely that you won't find out that your spouse or family member owned such a policy unless you check with credit card companies, banks, or any lenders to whom your spouse or family member owed money at the time of his or her death.

How do you file a life insurance benefit claim?

- Notify the insurance company that the policyholder has died: You should contact the insurance company as soon as possible. Call the policyholder services department directly. Or, if the life insurance policy was issued through an agent or an employer, ask them to notify the company for you to begin the claims process.
- File a claim form: You'll begin the claims process by filling out and signing a claimant's statement, and then attaching to it an original or certified copy of the policyholder's death cer-

tificate. If you are too distraught to fill out the form yourself, your insurance agent may fill it out for you, although you'll still have to sign it. If another beneficiary is named on the policy, that person must also fill out a claim form. You may also have to fill out IRS Form W-9 (Request for Taxpayer Identification Number and Certification), which will enable the insurance company to notify the IRS of any interest it has paid to you on the value of the policy. To expedite your claim, follow the insurance company's instructions carefully.

- Wait for the company to process the claim: Life insurance claims are usually paid quickly, often within a few days. First, however, the insurance company will ensure that you are the beneficiary of the policy, that the policy is current and in force, and that all conditions of the policy have been met. This is usually a simple matter and does not delay the claims process. Claims are more often delayed because the insurance company has not received a valid death certificate. The insurance company also has a right to contest (and perhaps deny) a claim if the insured died within two years following the purchase of the policy and the insurance company believes that there was fraud or a material misstatement made on the application.

How should you receive the life insurance proceeds?

Life insurance proceeds are often paid as lump-sum cash payments. Most people elect this form of payment because it enables them to control how the insurance money is invested or spent. In addition, if you elect to receive a lump-sum payment, you will not owe income tax on the life insurance proceeds.

Another way of receiving the proceeds of a life insurance policy is through a settlement option. Many types of settlement options are available for a beneficiary who is unable or unwilling to manage a lump sum of cash. Either the policyowner chooses the settlement option at the time he or she purchases the policy, or the beneficiary chooses the option at the time the benefit becomes payable (unless the policyowner had chosen an irrevocable option). You will find the available settlement options in the insurance policy.

Note: Some settlement option choices, such as payment as a life annuity, are irreversible. It may be best to take a lump-sum cash payment, put the money in the bank, and contact a qualified financial advisor.

APPENDIX 3

Long-Term Care Planning Checklist

GENERAL INFORMATION	YES	NO	N/A
1. Has relevant personal information been gathered? • Name • Date of birth • Legal state of residence • Health status, including medications being taken • Marital status • Family members available for support • Name, phone number, and address of attorney, physician, geriatric care manager or other advisor	☐	☐	☐
2. Has financial situation been assessed? • Income from Social Security, pension, employment, or other source • Expenses • Assets • Liabilities	☐	☐	☐

LONG-TERM CARE PLANNING	YES	NO	N/A
1. Is the need for long-term care imminent?	☐	☐	☐
2. Are assets sufficient to cover long-term care needs?	☐	☐	☐
3. Have ways to fund long-term care been reviewed/evaluated?	☐	☐	☐
4. If homeowner, has home equity as a use of funds been discussed?	☐	☐	☐
5. Are long-term care insurance benefits available?	☐	☐	☐
6. Have various housing options and their costs been considered? • In-home care • Living with a relative • Continuing care retirement community • Assisted living • Nursing home	☐	☐	☐
INSURANCE PLANNING	**YES**	**NO**	**N/A**
1. Is adequate health insurance available? • Medicare • Medigap • Private health insurance • Prescription plans	☐	☐	☐
2. Have Medicaid planning goals and strategies been considered?	☐	☐	☐

3. Has Medicaid qualification criteria been discussed?	☐	☐	☐
4. Has the need for long-term care insurance been established?	☐	☐	☐
5. Is long-term care insurance coverage available to the client?	☐	☐	☐
6. Have existing long-term care insurance policies been reviewed/evaluated?	☐	☐	☐
7. Does long-term care insurance coverage need to be upgraded?	☐	☐	☐
8. Do long-term care benefits need to be accessed?	☐	☐	☐
ESTATE PLANNING	**YES**	**NO**	**N/A**
1. Has long-term care planning been coordinated with estate planning needs?	☐	☐	☐
2. Have appropriate estate planning documents been prepared? • Will • Trust	☐	☐	☐
3. Have advanced medical directives been prepared? • Durable power of attorney • Living will • Health-care proxy	☐	☐	☐

4. Have letters of instruction been prepared?	☐	☐	☐
5. Has this information been communicated to family members?	☐	☐	☐
OTHER	**YES**	**NO**	**N/A**
1. Has the need for organizing important documents and records been discussed? • Bank account records (statements and passbooks) • Monthly bills to be paid • Stock certificates, bonds, and other investment records • Retirement plan statements • Real estate deeds, mortgages, and other property ownership records • Vehicle titles • Business agreements • Insurance policies • Will, trust, advanced medical directives, letters of instruction, and other documents • Birth certificate, marriage certificate, divorce decree, military service papers	☐	☐	☐
NOTES			